BEGGARS
AND
PRAYERS

BEGGARS AND PRAYERS

Adin Steinsaltz

RETELLS THE TALES OF

Rabbi Nachman of Bratslav

Translated by Yehuda Hanegbi, Herzlia Dobkin,
Deborah French, and Freema Gottlieb
Edited by Jonathan Omer-Man

Basic Books, Inc., Publishers   NEW YORK

Library of Congress Cataloging in Publication Data

Steinsaltz, Adin.
  Beggars and prayers.

  I. Tales, Hasidic. I. Nahman ben Simhah, of
Bratzlav, 1770?–1810? II. Title.
BM532.S73   296.8′33   78–54502
ISBN 0–465–00579–9 (cloth)
ISBN 0–465–00581–0 (paper)

Contents

Introduction

RABBI NACHMAN OF BRATSLAV (1772–1810), is one of the most original and outstanding thinkers to have emerged from the Hasidic world—a world that in its day was the source of a profound spiritual renaissance within Judaism, and that certainly did not lack for great men. Yet few of these actually attained the spiritual stature or the intellectual powers of Rabbi Nachman. In his short life, marked by physical and mental suffering, he not only produced several masterpieces of religious writing but also established a movement that remained faithful to his teaching and personal leadership both in his lifetime and after his death and, in fact, down to this very day.

Despite the passage of time and the changes in literary taste, his spiritual legacy has remained of fundamental significance to all who study the Hasidic way. Rabbi Nachman's Hasidim did their utmost to preserve his teachings, his talks, and his way of life. Both through his writings and through the tradition of his followers, there has come down to us a portrait of a truly remarkable man.

Of all Rabbi Nachman's works, the Tales, some of which appear in this volume, may be considered the peak of his creative life, both for the originality of their form and content and for the profundity of their underlying ideas. These stories, which are essentialy fairy tales dating from Nachman's last years, are a mixture of intellectual and poetic imagination, simplicity of form, and complexity of content.

On the one hand, any child can read them as one would a tale of ancient days, as the author himself put it; and, on the other hand, one can as an adult read them again and again, analyze and study them, and constantly discover in them layer upon layer of hitherto unrevealed symbol and meaning.

LIFE

Rabbi Nachman was born in April 1772, in the town of Medzhibozh in the Ukraine, to a distinguished Hasidic family. On his mother's side he was a great-grandson of Rabbi Israel Baal Shem Tov, the founder of Hasidism. Rabbi Nachman's outstanding qualities were already apparent from his earliest years; and although he was rather lively and something of a scamp, he seems to have possessed dazzling spiritual powers, incisive intelligence, and a genuine piety. It is said that his own childish sins would literally cause him to blush in shame before the Almighty.

In accordance with the custom of the times he was married off at the age of fourteen, and went to live at the house of his father-in-law in a village near the town of Medvedevka. There he remained for five years immersed in study and prayer. Desite his youth, people of all kinds gathered around him and chose him as their spiritual guide and teacher. Sometime before his twentieth birthday, he moved to town and was there acclaimed as a Hasidic rebbe with a substantial group of followers.

He thus emerged as the propounder of an original doctrine all his own which did not at all coincide with the teachings of many of the great Hasidic leaders of the day. This independence, combined with his youth and tendency to be outspoken in his criticism of important individuals, caused a growing disagreement which later resulted in Rabbi Nachman and his followers becoming isolated from other Hasidic groups.

In 1798, Nachman decided, quite suddenly, to travel to the Land of Israel, which throughout his life was for him a focal point of intellectual and deep emotional attraction. He felt, too, that by actually living in the Land he would accomplish what his great-grandfather, the Baal Shem Tov, had failed to do.

He therefore left his family and—accompanied only by his first pupil, who remained his faithful servant throughout his life—traveled via Odessa and Constantinople to the Holy Land. The journey was beset by hardship, mishaps, and strange incidents, all recorded by his companion. Rabbi Nachman decided to travel incognito and thus became the object of much hostility and suspicion along the way. His spiritual doubts and struggles, the odd way in which these manifested themselves, and the real hardships of the voyage —not the least of which was the fact that it took place at the time of Napoleon's march on the Holy Land—all added to the strange and mysterious quality of the journey. Notwithstanding, Rabbi Nachman managed to reach the Land of Israel and even to remain there for a few months, mainly at Tiberias and Safed. After several strange adventures, including his capture by the Turks and ransom by the Jewish community of Rhodes, he returned home.

Rabbi Nachman next settled in the town of Zlotopolye where, for reasons that are still not clear, he aroused the enmity of the charismatic Rabbi Leib (the Shpoler Zeide). This quarrel, and others like it, beset him throughout his life and caused him much grief wherever he went. He and his Hasidim, and their followers after them, were hounded by many leading rebbes of the day and in some places were actually persecuted. Rabbi Nachman was accused of arrogance, of Messianic pretensions, and of propagating semiheretical doctrines akin to Sabbatianism and Frankism. Although he himself tried to steer clear of taking an active part in these controversies, and although he had the support of such leaders as his powerful uncle, Baruch of Medzhibozh, the Seer of Lublin, and Rabbi Shnuer Zalman of Liadi, the opposition to his teachings continued. His supporters were far away, and anyway too preoccupied with their own struggles with the opponents of Hasidism, to give him any real support.

Nachman moved to the city of Bratslav in 1802 and lived there for several years. It was here that he produced the major part of his work. In Bratslav, he suffered several severe personal catastrophes: he was widowed; several of his children died—including his only son in whom he had invested his spiritual and dynastic hopes; and he himself was found to be suffering from tuberculosis. In 1810, he moved to Uman, knowing that his death was imminent; and he breathed his last there in October of that year. He died before he was forty years old.

STORIES, STUDENTS

Rabbi Nachman was a prolific writer and, from his youth, would write copious notes to himself, although he burnt almost as many as he wrote (most of his manuscripts were destroyed in the same way). Of the books he wrote himself, only one small volume remains—*Sefer Hamidot*—a collection of short proverbs or sayings arranged by subject (prayer, love, truth, and so on). Most of these proverbs are taken from ancient Jewish sources, ranging from the Bible itself to the later commentators. Rabbi Nachman did not just repeat these sayings but refashioned, simplified, and expanded them. *Sefer Hamidot* has appeared in many editions; and some scholars, such as Rabbi Tzadok HaCohen of Lublin and several of the Bratslav Hasidim, have added to them.

Rabbi Nachman's major work is *Lekutei Mohran,* published in 1808 and consisting of his teachings both public and individual over several years. The collection of sermons or talks is original and varied in both form and content, touching on almost every subject related to Judaism and Jewish thinking: ways of worshiping God, relations between man and his fellows, the Jews and other nations of the world, belief and doubt, and many more. The talks are based on texts drawn from the Bible, the Talmud, and the Zohar; and Rabbi Nachman builds a whole repertoire of new meanings into each and every word—a multidimensional series of mystic implications and exegesis. The book, which found warm support among the religious leaders of the day, is an outstanding demonstration of Rabbi Nachman's mastery of the sources, and his effortless linking of subjects from many areas. *Lekutei Mohran* is the source text of the Bratslav Hasidim; and they, their descendants, and many others have found in it—each in his own way—Torah, wisdom, and guidance.

The Tales, like the second part of *Lekutei Mohran,* were published posthumously; and most of them, especially the longer stories, were recounted to his Hasidim in the last years of Nachman's life. They are told in the language of the people, in Yiddish, and were recorded by his outstanding pupil, Rabbi Nathan, who added to them from memory or from his own notes, where necessary, and translated and published them, initially, in Hebrew. (Subsequent editions were published in accordance with Rabbi Nachman's wishes in a bilingual Hebrew-Yiddish translation.) As well as the major books, three volumes relating to Rabbi Nachman were published: *Conversations of Rabbi Nachman, In Praise of Rabbi Nachman,* and *The Life of Rabbi Nachman.* These are not merely biographies but recount his teachings as they were delivered orally on various occasions, and are crucial to an understanding of his work.

Over the years some dozens of volumes have appeared on Rabbi Nachman—most of them new versions or anthologies of the earlier works, although some do contain new material attributed to Nachman himself.

Rabbi Nachman's pupils and followers are worthy of a chapter to themselves. As we have seen, he was blessed from his earliest years with a gift for attracting people who not only learned Torah and good deeds with him but were bound to him by deep ties that could not be broken even by isolation and persecution. The "Bratslavers" were a heterogenous community, including learned rabbis, teachers, and scholars as well as simple folk, some from the lowest strata of society; and Rabbi Nachman was noted for his ability to find a common language with each and every one. At the same time, his personal preference was for superior people, people whom he felt were more likely to understand the depth and scope of his ideas and—what is more—to disseminate them further. The outstanding personality in this category is his closest pupil and follower, Rabbi Nathan Sternharz. Rabbi Nathan came from a wealthy and respected family and, like Nachman, was from his youth recognized as a prodigious talent. He came to Rabbi Nachman in 1802; and from the very first moment of their meeting, the two found a deep bond of communication and understanding. As Rabbi Nachman said at the time, "We have already known each other but had simply separated for a time." It was Rabbi Nathan who collected, anthologized, and published Nachman's works; and were it not for his devoted labors, it is doubtful whether Nachman's literary work would have survived to the extent that it has.

All Rabbi Nachman's books and the first books written about him are the fruits of Rabbi Nathan's devotion. Much more than an editor and compiler, he was also a creative writer in his own right and actually added to and developed Rabbi Nachman's teaching. Rabbi Nathan's book *Lekutei Tefillot* (Collection of Prayers) is in itself a remarkable poetic creation, a passionate devotional work produced in response to Rabbi Nachman's wishes that his teachings should be expressed as prayer.

Rabbi Nathan's creative powers are particularly evident in his great book *Lekutei Halachot*—a series of mystical or kabbalistic discourses on Halacha (Jewish canon law) in which he not only draws on Rabbi Nachman but expands on him in a brilliant, original commentary.

Rabbi Nathan succeeded Rabbi Nachman as leader of the Bratslav Hasidim, although such was his devotion to his teacher's memory that he steadfastly refused to become the rebbe of the community but rather retained the status of pupil of his great master. Hence, the unique characteristic of the Bratslav Hasidim down to the present time: they are a Hasidic court with no living rebbe but regard themselves as the direct followers of the irreplaceable Rabbi Nachman.

Rabbi Nachman began to relate the Tales in 1806. Each one was told spontaneously, usually after a relevant talk or sermon. The greatest, and the most significant, were told during his last years; and the most important of all, "The Seven Beggars," just half a year before his death. Hasidic literature is rich in stories and anecdotes, but Nachman's Tales have quite a different quality. The Hasidic story usually relates to specific individuals (usually leading personalities of the movement), their deeds, righteousness, sanctity, wonders that befell them, or words of wisdom. Rabbi Nachman's tales, on the other hand, have a distinctive form and thus became a vehicle for his teachings and ideas on various issues, in the form of myths or legends. In terms of structure, they are similar to folk or fairy tales, Jewish and non-

Jewish. They do not fall into the category of *belles lettres* like the mythic stories of Hans Christian Andersen, Oscar Wilde, Franz Kafka (whose work has much in common with Nachman's), Hermann Hesse, and others. These literary fairy tales, like other literary works in general, are intended to express ideas, portray characters, and serve as a vehicle for poetic and symbolic language. But Nachman's stories include highly compressed and clearly defined Torah teaching—just as do his other works—expressed in literary and poetic form. Thus, the Tales are simply a more literary, sophisticated means of presenting the teachings; and form, or even plot, is not used as an end in itself. Rabbi Nachman himself well understood the significance of the literary form he had chosen. He said, "From now on I will tell you tales," adding that he believed that thus he would be better able to explain his teachings in a more profound and penetrating way. At the same time he also gave explicit Torah teachings (*Lekutei Mohran, Patah R. Shimon*) in which he outlined his approach. He was wont to say that no one is capable of absorbing explicit Torah teachings without some loss of meaning, and that therefore the inner content has to be given form by means of tales and stories. As he put it, when the blind man is healed, one must protect him from the sudden glare of light: the inner face of truth must be disguised lest it be distorted or harmfully misunderstood; and the true scholar disguises the inner meaning of his teachings according to the level of his hearers. Rabbi Nachman ends this discourse with the words: "But then there is one who fell so deeply asleep until he could not be roused except by tales of ancient days from which all seventy faces of the Torah receive their being."

Rabbi Nachman's stories, which he himself called *Tales of Ancient Days,* are therefore a medium for conveying the hidden aspects of Torah in all its multifaceted dress, albeit in such a veiled way that the content is not outwardly apparent; therefore, anyone can accept and achieve some kind of enrichment and enlightenment from it.

The Tales are few in number. Thirteen of varying lengths make up the main body of work; some shorter tales were also added as was also, at a later date, a long story, doubtfully attributed to Rabbi Nachman; while another handful may be found scattered throughout his various works. Although they are so few, the tales are not uniform in literary style or in content. For instance, the story "The Clever Man and the Simple Man" expresses a straightforward idea in a unique narrative style. "The Losing of the King's Daughter" appears to be an adaptation of a folk tale, while "The Merchant and the Pauper" is pure allegory. Some of the stories, such as "The Master of Prayer" and "The Seven Beggars," are extremely complex—tales within tales within tales. In some cases, the story itself is well known, and only the change in emphasis gives it its special quality. Elsewhere, the plot is totally original from start to finish and has no parallel outside Rabbi Nachman's own creative world. Generally speaking, he then used literary form not as an end in itself but as a means of expressing ideas. However, in everything relating to the details of the story itself, in its substantive adaptation, in the use of language no less than in the development of the story, he is meticulous. Although he may depart from the subject at hand to raise another idea or to sketch in a new image, these departures are worked out to their minutest detail and carefully woven into the central theme, which in all Nachman's Tales has but one objective: to pass on his ideas. The sources from which these details of plot and tale are drawn are many and varied: Kabbalah, folk tales, Bible and Halacha, history and contemporary events all served him as raw material.

This multiplicity of form and content have an additional, more spiritual meaning. Nachman himself has said that they try to "express the seventy faces of the Torah"; and indeed, in many instances, one may discern more than one meaning and even several layers of meaning. Most of these are not contradictory but show different facets and aspects of one fundamental idea. It therefore happens that various details within one story do not relate to the same level of meaning. Here, too, we can see the parallel between the Tales and Rabbi Nachman's sermons; for in *Lekutei Mohran,* too, the subject subdivides into several sub-issues, each one of which is dealt with separately. Eventually all these elements combine in the general structure.

KABBALISTIC SOURCES

The fundamental key to Rabbi Nachman's Tales is to be found in the Kabbalah. Almost all the tales—in terms of form and content, symbolism and imagery, heroes and poetic touches—are taken from Kabbalah, especially the Book of the Zohar and the teachings of Rabbi Luria, the holy "Ari" (1534–1572). This use is sometimes veiled by the imaginative structure or by a seemingly realistic description in which the kabbalistic symbols are not particularly evident. Elsewhere, especially in the last tales, which are highly complex in both content and structure, their source is plainly evident. That is to say, Rabbi Nachman takes symbols that have a clear and unequivocal meaning in Kabbalah and weaves them into a perfect homiletic story.

The main difference between kabbalistic-symbolic literature generally and the symbolic form of Nachman's stories lies in the life and human vitality that Nachman gives these conventional symbols.

In kabbalistic literature, the use of symbols is stylized, and the various images serve almost as mathematical formulae. In the Tales, they become creatures of flesh and blood with human qualities and failings. Not only do the king, the queen, and the king's daughter appear in the tales in their clear kabbalistic meaning, but they are balanced by a meticulous attention to even the minutest details of the story. Nachman himself rightly pointed out that in this sense his stories are precise not only in their broad allegorical structure but also in their finest details. His literary work is not impressionistic but precise, similar to a Breughel painting, where even the seemingly trivial or scarcely seen detail is portrayed as exactly as the central figures themselves.

FOLK SOURCES

Most fairy tales are presented as folk tales—from the opening formula "Once upon a time . . ." down to the intentionally simplistic and stylistic details. Rabbi Nachman not only makes use of this literary genre *per se* but also draws heavily on existing folk tales. He himself was aware of this use. His follower has said:

Before he told the first tale in this book, he said: "The fairy tales of the world hold many hidden and exalted things, but they have become distorted because they are deficient and [people have become] confused and no longer tell them properly—putting the beginning at the end and the other way around. Now the Baal Shem Tov could create divine unities by means of a story. When he saw that the heavenly channels had been disrupted he would correct them by means of a tale." (Quoted from Rabbi Nathan's foreword to the Tales.)

As a dedicated Hasid, Rabbi Nachman believed that the whole world in all its details is paralleled by an upper world, and that therefore tales and songs that men recount and sing are directed toward higher things, although the tellers themselves do not realize this. In the very same way, the leaders of the Hasidic movement also worked with folk songs, Jewish and non-Jewish, linking them to their own inner content. The use of folk tales is, according to Rabbi Nachman's theory, not only an exploitation of familiar material but an action that is in itself a *tikkun,* or "repair," of the world; raising up the divine sparks which are imprisoned in the banality of the world, and thereby bringing about their redemption by means of their purposeful, intentional, and meaningful use. However, Rabbi Nathan presented only a few of his teachers' *tikkunim* and adaptations of folk tales because he dealt mainly with the original stories; and even here, where the plots are novel and original, we find extracts from well-known fairy stories that Rabbi Nachman combined with his own tales. In a way, it is precisely in these ancient stories that his creative gift becomes evident: the same small details that he adds, omits, arranges, or alters reveal his special touch which can turn a common folk tale into a kabbalistic allegory.

BIBLICAL AND TALMUDIC SOURCES

Rabbi Nachman had a deep and wide knowledge of the scriptures, as is outstandingly evident in all his writings. In all his work, and especially in the Tales, he uses these sources in a special way, blessed as he was not only with great poetic imagination and a powerful feeling for great symbology, but also with a great felicity of word imagery. Most people take the imagery and idiom of their own tongue for granted. Nachman, on the other hand, not only saw this imagery in its conventional meaning but was able to give these "figures of speech" life in clear visual and even spatial terms. When he read the Bible, the whole galaxy of figures sprang into life and motion. Verses, paragraphs, and sometimes even whole chapters became tales in his eyes. In fact, we find this view of the Bible in much of kabbalistic literature; while Nachman, in the Tales as elsewhere, went beyond this to creative development of the original. An outstanding example may be found in "The Master of Prayer." This almost concrete use of language is not unknown in literature generally but is most evident among painters: many of Chagall's works are simply pictures of figures of speech.

DREAMS

Another source for at least some of Nachman's Tales seems to have been his dreams. We cannot, of course, know which of the stories have their roots here; and it is sure that these, too, were adapted and "processed" by him. At the same time, it seems that several stories (in particular "The Fly and the Spider," which does not appear in this collection) are simply adaptations of dreams.

Other rebbes also recounted complex and highly significant dreams, and some even made a practice of recording their night visions (see, for instance, *Megillat Setarim* by Rabbi Itzhak of Komarno or *Rissesei Lilah* [Dew of Night] by Rabbi Tzadok HaCohen). Rabbi Nachman himself did recount some of his dreams to his followers and, had he had time, probably would have turned some of them into finished tales. Literary adaptations of some of these dreams are extant—at least two of them from the pen of I. L. Peretz.

AUTOBIOGRAPHICAL AND HISTORICAL

A large part of Rabbi Nachman's output was autobiographical, for he contemplated his own life and spoke a great deal about his experiences and thoughts. This tendency is consistent with his attitude toward confession, and his followers would indeed confess to him and, eventually, to each other. Nachman particularly stressed the human need to pour out one's heart before God not only in formal prayers but in a personal "conversation" in which one tells Him of one's spiritual and material problems. This teaching became one of the fundamentals of the Bratslav way. It is not therefore surprising that a great deal of Nachman's teachings are a chain of personal tales and confessions. Thus, not only in his Torah teaching (where he often spoke of himself and the problems in his soul) but in his stories, too, there is some kind of transfer of his private problems, even though the discussion is on a general, objective level. Every literary or artistic work is actually partly autobiographical or contains a measure of confession, and often this is what gives it its power. For this reason, there is an exaggerated attempt on the part of some researchers to stress the personal, private side of Nachman's oeuvre. He himself was aware of this aspect of his work and would often take care to separate the personal from the general. The public teachings no less than the Tales hint at his personality and deeds—although, according to his view of things, the function of these experiences was to bring people to a better general understanding of what he wanted to convey. The private act, his own or anyone else's, for him hinted at the worlds above, and each man could find, within his own life, all the worlds. "In my flesh I shall see God" (Job 19:26) is a principle of Kabbalah stressed by all the various schools of Hasidism. This is why we find in the Tales many things that are directly connected with events in Nachman's own life, and many of the characters, heroes, and subsidiary figures are reflections of aspects of Nachman's personality (the "lad" in "The Merchant and the Pauper," the eponymous hero in "The Master of Prayer," and so on).

Many tales also expressed Rabbi Nachman's explicit response to events and occurrences. He himself said that some of his tales hold the key to things he had done in the past or had happened in his life. The selection of characters was therefore intentional and conscious; while in the adaptation of personages and events to Torah teaching or a tale, they underwent a process of abstraction and generalization. Nachman saw himself as a symbol, as the hero of a story of cosmic significance.

In some of the Tales, we find not only an "event in time" that gives the story its dynamics, but also veiled hints at real personalities, whether drawn from Rabbi Nachman's own personal circle or a historical figure from Biblical times or later. Nachman also showed great interest (even though we today cannot always follows his allusions) in world news and events. "The King's Son and the Son of the Maid" was told after a discourse on the Emperor Napoleon. He often mentions personalities of various sorts, such as Christopher Columbus; while elsewhere—as in "The Master of Prayer" —there are references to specific events, past and present.

FORM AND CONTENT

When Rabbi Nachman told his stories orally, he expressed the desire that they should be published as a book, and even described the form this book should take, sensing or knowing that the Tales were not only an expression of his teachings but also works of art. He said, "My thought is to publish a book of tales and it will be written with the upper part [of the page] in the Holy Tongue [Hebrew] with a Yiddish translation below." He added, "And what can the world do with these Tales? Well, after all, they are nice fables."

This substantive relationship between form and content is one of the fundamental goals of these fables. From the outset, they were intended as "Pleasant Tales"—to be read for pleasure, even entertainment; while their inner content with its many meanings must function not only openly by means of a concerted effort but also in such a way that the reader himself cannot always account for the fact that a given tale has affected him so greatly. Nachman's first story, "The Losing of the King's Daughter," originally opened with these words: "On the way I told a tale which caused all who heard it to begin to think on repentance." And this, in fact, was also the way of the Baal Shem Tov: to tell tales of multidimensional significance so that whoever heard them, even if ignorant of their symbolism, would still get something out of them.

The ability of these tales to "awaken from the sleep of seventy faces" lies in this duality of form and content. The story told in this way is so weighted with significance that it forces the hearer to think on it again and again and to search for its general and personal meaning—to arouse man to greater things.

LANGUAGE AND TRANSLATIONS

The Tales were originally told in Yiddish, but Rabbi Nathan wrote them down in Hebrew, and they were originally published in that language. But, in subsequent editions, the author's wishes were carried out, and bilingual Yiddish versions were published—Hebrew on the upper part of the page, Yiddish below.

In the Hebrew version, Rabbi Nathan tried to preserve and duplicate the exact speech of the author in all its precise nuances; the text is therefore somewhat choppy and not always as clear as it could be. Rabbi Nathan actually apologized for the ungrammatical style ("coarse language," he dubbed it) used in order to remain as faithful as possible to the original.

The Tales were translated into many languages, and the Hebrew versions underwent many adaptations. Successive editors and translators tried to improve or even adorn the language and style and to make the story line read more smoothly—thus causing the very thing Rabbi Nathan had striven hard to avoid: embellishments of form and polishing of plot; even the slightest changes or omissions brought about subtle (and not so subtle) changes in meaning. It must be remembered that these stories were the product of a brilliant literary and intellectual creativity and that each tale was carefully worked out, with the interweaving of the small details into the overall framework leading to a specific and definite meaning.

For this reason, translations and adaptations that alter the form, even in the slightest degree, often disrupt the meaning of the content. An outstanding example is the translation by Martin Buber which is frequently an overly free adaptation of the original, in which the omissions and changes cause significant and sometimes deliberate distortion. This present translation is based on Rabbi Adin Steinsaltz's Hebrew edition of the Tales (Tel Aviv: Dvir, 1981), a text that diverged slightly from Rabbi Nathan's Hebrew version, relying to a large extent on original source materials and, in many instances, on comparisons with the early

Yiddish text. Although not the original that so many researchers believe it to be, this is by no means a secondary translation, as it is based upon a faithful record of the Tales handed down by Rabbi Nachman's closest follower who must have had vivid memories of hearing his rebbe at first hand. Changes have inevitably resulted from the transfer from one language to another; and it is, of course, not always possible to find the exact word or phrase in all its most precise nuances—especially when translating from Hebrew and Yiddish, languages rich in associative idioms.

There is no doubt that the English reader loses some of the vivid word images and combinations of the original. This loss is heightened when one remembers that almost 250 years separate us from Rabbi Nachman with all the consequent change in language use, attitude, and life experience.

The slight roughness and simplicity of form and language, and the details of content, have here been preserved as far as possible and serve not only to introduce the English reader to the contents and meaning of the Tales but also to convey something of their tone and feeling.

COMMENTARY

All Rabbi Nachman's Tales (even the simplest of them) are highly significant and most of them are complex allegories. As already noted, the Tales were intended at the outset to have several dimensions. However, the commentary is not meant to be an exhaustive exploration of the whole treasury of meaning. Precise analysis and exhaustive commentary (even if these are possible, for we often lack the necessary tools for this task) would be a highly technical undertaking, requiring great resources of time, effort, and manpower. For this reason, each tale in the collection has a commentary dealing with the tale's fundamental issue—in accordance with comparisons with kabbalistic and Hasidic texts and Rabbi Nachman's own works. Other strata of meaning (whether in relation to the whole tale or part of it) are sometimes hinted at in the body of the commentary; but the reader should bear in mind that, within the framework of this book, it is not desirable to penetrate the depths of all these things and to analyze all the details, so that many issues are merely alluded to or mentioned in passing. Often one may see in the different parts of a single story two different subject themes, each one belonging to a different meaning level or to different viewpoints of the story. The explanations are by way of being notes on a general framework of ideas intended to direct the reader in his search for "the gate to the seventy faces of Torah."

Although the Tales are outstanding for their complex and complicated symbolism, some of these symbols are standard and regular, because Rabbi Nachman's symbolic system is not an expression of his personal, private world but belongs to the whole body of Jewish and kabbalistic thought. Although Rabbi Nachman often gives a distinctive explanation and adds his own special contribution, this is an inseparable part of a long tradition of Jewish thinking in general and of Hasidic thinking in particular. Thus, the selection of the fundamental symbols was not arbitrary or by chance but inevitably derived from Rabbi Nachman's Hasidic sources and ways of thinking, on which he built. Moreover, Rabbi Nachman's Tales deal not with the whole range of Jewish thought but with specific aspects of it; and, obviously, there is an inner and external connection between the stories— although the plot varies greatly from tale to tale. Most of the stories have one general theme: the problem of the *tikkun* ("repair") of the world and its way to redemption.

Our world is the world of exile, an imperfect world, almost impenetrable by the Divine light. The goal of the Jewish people (especially its leaders and righteous souls and, above all, the Messiah) is to redeem this world and to perfect it. Therefore, most of Rabbi Nachman's stories deal with various aspects of these fundamental issues. In some stories, the subject is universal; in others, it is connected to the individual struggle of man's soul; in others, the specific issue of the Messiah is raised; but all the stories complement each other and together make up a single cycle, whose central theme is the problem of the crisis of the world and its redemption.

THE KING

In most of Rabbi Nachman's stories, the king (or emperor) symbolizes God—as is usually plain to see in context. Whenever a story speaks of one king, a supreme king who is ruler over all, the meaning is the King of Kings. In Jewish tradition, this is one of the most ancient symbols of all, occurring in the Torah itself, in the teachings of the Prophets, and in the Psalms. In the Talmud and the homiletic teachings (Midrash), it is also a standard symbol: a text beginning "Parable of a King" almost always refers to God; and this finds its inevitable reflection in the Kabbalah and in Hasidism also.

The most outstanding aspect of Rabbi Nachman's Tales is the symbolic imagery of the King, and it is a paradoxical fact that He is almost always portrayed outside the actual framework of the plot itself. The King, with whom so many of the Tales begin, is not the hero of the story and may even be the "king who died" or the "king who was." This fact need not surprise us. According to the reality characteristic of the subject Rabbi Nachman deals with, God is not actively revealed within the world. The Creator who is the Prime Cause of all life is not revealed within the ugly world of exile and fall, and the very fact that the world is in a state of exile derives from God's not being revealed in it. On the contrary, the world in which the king is revealed as King of the Universe, and which He actively rules, is the world redeemed: the perfected world. The creation of the world and the giving of free will to man are, in a certain sense, the beginning of *Hester Panim,* or Divine withdrawal (literally, "concealing the Face"), until it seems that God "hath forsaken the earth" (Ezekiel 8:12). Therefore, God acts from a position of withdrawal although this action is not manifest or seen, and herein lies the major thrust of the Tales. The choice of returning to a state of revelation—redemption—is given to mankind generally and to the Jewish people in particular. For this reason it is not the king who is the active factor in the Tales, but rather the people who go in search of him.

Thus, in most of the stories, the king creates the basic situation; and from that point on, the hero is charged with bringing about the *tikkun,* or repair, of the world. According to Kabbalah, God Himself (the Infinite One Blessed Be He) acts in the world by means of the ten *Sefirot* (attributes or emanations of the Divine) that characterize His revelation as Creator and Prime Mover. The essence that lies beyond these revelations (from the Supreme Crown onward) is the "void," and He Himself is hidden: "Verily thou art a God that hidest thyself, O God of Israel" (Isaiah 45:15); "At the brightness that was before him his thick clouds passed" (Psalms 18:12). As the Baal Shem Tov explained many times, the revelation that God is to be found within that concealment, is itself the solution, the redemption expressed as "they shall see eye to eye" (Isaiah 52:8).

THE KING'S DAUGHTER

The king's daughter is a frequent image in the Tales. She, too, is usually used in a single symbolic sense—that of the *Shekhinah,* understanding of which is one of the fundamental issues in kabbalistic literature. It may be said that the equation, "The Holy One Blessed Be He is the *Shekhinah*" is the principle foundation of the relationship between God and the world.

In the most basic way, the *Shekhinah* is the immanence of the Divine Power in this world and that which vivifies it. The *Shekhinah* is the Divine emanation which pours forth on the world, the inner breath of life of the universe. And since the *Shekhinah* is the essence of the life of the world, it is clear that "She" has names, appellations, and revelations without number—because, in a certain sense, the existence of the world is only one specific aspect of the *Shekhinah.* In the Kabbalah, the *Shekhinah* is the emanation usually called "Sovereignty," because she is the Sovereign power of God in the world and therefore, as well as being a female figure, is the recipient of Divine Abundance. She is called the "King's Daughter."

Sovereignty, or the *Shekhinah,* has another side: it is also the Community of Israel in its spiritual sense—the source of all the souls of Israel, the source in which all the souls exist as a single unit. In another sense, it is the source of power, the communal soul of all Israel. The use of these interpretations of the *Shekhinah* are found throughout the scriptures; and the images of Israel as woman, bride, daughter, or beloved are found in the Torah, in the Prophets, and in Jewish literature generally throughout the generations.

The fall of the world, and its receding from the awareness

of its link to the Divine and to the exile and fall of Israel, are the exile of the *Shekhinah;* and redemption is "raising the *Shekhinah* from the dust." As stated, all of Jewish literature abounds in symbols, parables, and images of the *Shekhinah,* all of which blend to produce poetic forms that can be interpreted in many ways. Two images are particularly frequent: the *Shekhinah* as the Bride of God or, according to the concept of the Song of Songs, the Beloved of God; or the Bride as the King's Daughter, with Israel as the Bridegroom (a figure frequently found in the homiletic Midrash Aggadah). The two images combine in a wonderfully subtle fashion in the song sung to welcome the Sabbath "Lecha Dodi" ("Beloved Come to meet the Bride"), in which inner content is generated by the transition from one meaning to another.

In the Tales, wherever the king's daughter is mentioned, the reference is to the *Shekhinah* as the soul of the world, the soul of Israel, and the link between Israel and the Messiah. In any case, it should be remembered that the number of images, symbols, and parables bound up together is very large; and although Rabbi Nachman makes overt use of some of them, he more often merely hints at their deeper significance, which perhaps can be fully understood only by referring to the inner meaning of the Tales.

THE SHATTERING OF THE VESSELS

The world in general and the Jewish world in particular are not perfected at this time but await redemption—the removal of the barriers and the veil that separate Divine existence in the world. The same crisis points in which we find this "withdrawal" are one of the central issues of Kabbalah. These crisis points are historically sequential, and all follow the same basic pattern: the fall from a higher to a lower state, from a stage of relative perfection to a fall that is never final, whose outcome is always a new ascent—indeed, sometimes the fall is necessary in order to rise again. Each crisis, because of this inner similarity, may be represented by the same images, which, although certainly not identical, are all connected.

We may identify four major crises in "cosmic history." The first precedes Creation and is actually the means of Creation of our world, with the Divine withdrawal, with the fact of its being "world" in all its entirety. This crisis is called the "Shattering of the Vessels," a concept dominant in Lurianic kabbalism. Put simply, the higher forces "fell and shattered" before the Creation of the world. Some are the Divine Sparks of which our world is partly formed; while others fell so far that they became trapped in the world's matter and thus support its physical being, including the evil in it. The perfect redemption of these sparks is the purpose of man's existence and of Israel's existence in particular.

The second crisis is the Sin of the Tree of Knowledge—the fall of Adam, the first man, from the perfection of Eden to the confusion and disruption of our world in which the distinction between good and evil has become blurred. This is the fall common to all mankind.

Next comes the Sin of the Golden Calf. After the spiritual exaltation of the Giving of the Torah (in itself a return to Eden), the Jewish nation goes astray and worships the idol of the Golden Calf, thus forfeiting its uniqueness as a vessel for the perfect transmission of the laws of the world and, as a result, must find its way to redemption, for itself and for others.

The fourth crisis is the Destruction of the Temple, which was also by way of being an element of Eden, a transition to the created world. Since the Destruction, the *Shekhinah* itself is in exile and is no longer revealed at any particular point in this world.

The exile of the *Shekhinah,* like the Shattering of the Vessels, opens the way to the forces of evil that derive their strength from Her strength, until it is they who visibly become the ruling force in our world, while sanctity and holiness, the holiness and sanctity of Israel, are in exile, withdrawn into obscurity. The *Shekhinah* in exile is not only withdrawn in that She is unrevealed and unknown, and that "Her feet go down to death" (Proverbs 5:5), but she actually becomes the force that feeds the evil in the world. Man's sins, Israel's sin, increase this "withdrawal" in the sense that "I have sinned and He is bound in chains."

In Rabbi Nachman's Tales, the fall is portrayed by several images, of which the outstanding is the lost king's daughter hunted and hounded—the *Shekhinah* in exile. And since the various stages of the fall are internally connected, it is not surprising that several events occurring at different times are portrayed in one allegorical description, which is compacted with other elements and aspects which all complement and fulfill each other.

HEROES

As in most stories, Rabbi Nachman's heroes are solitary men; and since they are at the same time both fictional and symbolic figures, and since their symbolism is also wide ranging, they are not simple individuals either. Like the figures of the Bible and the Kabbalah, they are multifaceted, not just private personages but also archetypes. The sages held that the acts of the fathers are an indication to the sons (a notion that Nachmanides developed into a unique system of commentary on Biblical personalities); and it is a fact that, in Jewish literature, even historical figures are part of a universal symbolic world: "We find in man that which we find in the world." In kabbalistic literature in particular, Biblical figures are symbolically associated with the specific emanations or attributes of God, called the *Sefirot,* particularly the seven "shepherds"—leaders—of Israel. Thus, in order of appearance: Abraham is grace; Itzhak, might; Yaacov, splendor; Yosef, root or foundation; Moses, eternity (and also knowledge); Aaron, majesty; David (and also Rachel), sovereignty. In Rabbi Nachman's Tales, too, the characters often represent a specific attribute of the Divine.

The relationship between man and the world, the fact that man is a little world in himself, is one of the most fundamental concepts of Kabbalah. In Hasidic literature, this idea was strongly emphasized and appears in many forms, from a view of the Torah as man's world (Rabbi Yosef of Polonnoye, a follower of the Baal Shem Tov) to a view of the precise relations between the soul and the *Sefirot* which is highly developed in the literature of the Habad movement. The same idea occurs frequently in Rabbi Nachman's work, and several of his stories can be understood both in universal human terms and also as a theory of events occurring within the soul. These commentaries do not contradict each other but are complementary.

The *Shekhinah* is also the communal soul *(Knesset Israel)* of the nation and, in a sense, is also the highest soul of every Jew. The loss, seeking out, and eventual redemption of the *Shekhinah* is the private experience of sin and separation from God, which is paralleled by the universal experience of exile and redemption.

Thus, Rabbi Nachman's heroes are sometimes universal and struggle for the being of the whole world, and sometimes they are righteous *Tzaddikim* working for redemption in the Jewish context; elsewhere they are the individual powers working within the soul; and sometimes they are all of these things together.

Glossary

Baal Shem Tov. Appellation of Israel ben Eliezer (c. 1700–1760), founder of the hasidic movement and great-grandfather of Rabbi Nachman of Bratslav.

Halakhah. The body of Jewish law.

Kabbalah. The Jewish mystical and esoteric tradition.

Knesset Israel. An ancient concept denoting the soul of the entire Jewish people; according to the Kabbalah, an aspect of the *Shekhinah*.

Midrash. Narrative and exegetical material found in the Talmud and other works.

Mitzvot. The commandments given to the Jewish people in the Torah as elucidated in later works; taken together, the *Mitzvot* form the basis of *Halakhah*.

Sefirot. The ten; a kabbalistic term referring to the aspects or attributes of God, by means of which divinity acts upon and is manifest in the world; as opposed to the infinite and unknowable aspects of divinity.

Shekhinah. The last of the ten *Sefirot*, the mode in which God is described as present in the world. Generally defined as being in exile in the world.

Talmud. The greatest body of postbiblical Jewish literature, produced between 200 and 500 C.E.

Torah. The five books of Moses.

Zaddik. Literally, a righteous person; in Hasidism, a great spiritual leader.

Zohar. The major and central work of the Kabbalah.

BEGGARS
AND
PRAYERS

The Losing of the King's Daughter

ONCE there was a king. He had six sons and one daughter. The daughter was very precious to him. He was very fond of her and used to play with her. One day when they were together, he was annoyed at her, and the words flew from his lips, "May the evil one take you!"

That night she went to her room, and in the morning no one knew where she was. Her father, the king, was very distressed, and he sought her everywhere. On seeing that the king was in great sorrow, the king's chamberlain asked to be given a servant, a horse, and money for expenses, and he went to look for her. He searched for a very long time until he found her.

He journeyed through deserts, fields, and forests. Once when he was traveling in the desert, he saw a side path. He decided that, since he had been in the desert for such a long time and had not found her, he should try that path, and perhaps he would reach a town or village. He went on for a long time, and in the end he saw a castle and many soldiers standing guard all around it.

The castle was beautiful and finely laid out, with well-trained guards. He was afraid that the guards would not let him in. But he decided, "I shall take the risk." So he left the horse and went up to the castle. He was allowed to go in— no one hindered him—and he went from room to room. He came to a great hall and saw a king wearing his crown and many soldiers standing about. Many musicians were playing their instruments before the king, and it was all very beautiful and fine. And neither the king nor anyone else there asked him anything. He saw good food there, and he went and ate. Then he went and lay down in a corner, to watch what was happening. He saw the king order that the queen be brought, and servants went to bring her. Then there was a great commotion and much joy, and the musicians played and sang when she was brought. A throne was brought for her, and she was seated next to the king. The chamberlain saw her and recognized her. It was the lost daughter of his king.

Then the queen looked around and saw someone lying in the corner, and she recognized him. She got up and went over to him, and then she touched him and asked, "Do you recognize me?"

He answered, "Yes, I recognize you—you are the king's daughter who was lost." He asked her, "How do you come to be here?"

She answered, "Because of the words that flew from my father's lips, that the evil one take me. This is the evil one's place."

He told her that her father was grief-stricken and had been looking for her for many years. Then he asked her, "How can I get you out of here?"

She answered, "You cannot, unless you choose a place and remain there for a year, and for the entire year you yearn to get me out of here. Whenever you have a free moment, you must do nothing but yearn for me and hope to get me out of here. And on the last day of the year, you must fast and not sleep for twenty-four hours."

So he went away and did all that she said. At the end of the year, on the last day, he fasted and did not sleep all night. Then he got up and went to the king's daughter, to take her away. On the way he saw a tree on which fine apples were growing, and he was filled with longing, and he ate one of them. As soon as he ate the apple, he fell down, and a deep sleep overcame him. He slept for a very long time. His servant shook him but could not rouse him. Then, when he awoke, he asked the servant, "Where am I in the world?"

The servant told him the whole story: "You have been sleeping for many years. I kept myself alive by eating the fruit."

He was grief-stricken and went back to the king's daughter. She was in great sorrow and said, "Because of one day, because you could not restrain yourself for one day and you ate the apple, you have lost everything. Had you come on that day, you would have taken me out of here. True, it is difficult not to eat, especially on the last day, when the evil impulse is so strong. Go, therefore, and choose yourself another place and remain there for a year. On the last day you may eat, but you must not slumber; and you must drink no wine, lest you fall asleep. The main thing is sleep."

He went away and did what she said. On the last day, he returned to her. On the way he saw a flowing spring. It was red, and its smell was the smell of wine. He said to his servant, "Look, there is a spring, and water should be flowing from it, but it is red, and its smell is the smell of wine." And he went and tasted a little of the spring, and immediately he fell down and slept for seventy years.

While he was sleeping, many soldiers marched past, and their baggage trains went after them. The servant hid himself from the soldiers. Then a carriage went past, and the king's daughter was in it. She stepped down and sat next to the chamberlain. She recognized him and tried to rouse him, but he did not wake up. She then began to complain: that after all the troubles and tribulations, after all the years that he had spent trying to get her away, "because of one day, on which you might have succeeded, you have lost everything." And she wept a great deal and said, "It's a great pity for you and for me. I have been here for such a long time, and I cannot get away." Then she took a kerchief from her head, and she wrote on it with her tears and left it by his side, and she rose and seated herself in the carriage and drove away.

When he woke up, he asked the servant, "Where am I in the world?"

The servant told him the whole story: how many soldiers had marched past, and then a carriage had gone by, and the king's daughter had stepped down and had wept over him, and that she had said that it was a great pity for both of them.

He looked about him and saw the kerchief lying nearby. He asked, "Where is this from?"

The servant answered, "She left it here and wrote on it with her tears."

So he took the kerchief and raised it to the sun, and he began to see letters, and then he read what was written: about her complaints and her weeping, and that she was no longer in the same castle, and he should search for a golden mountain on which stood a castle of pearl, "and there you will find me."

He left the servant and went off by himself to search for her. He searched for several years. Then he thought, "In places where men dwell one cannot find a golden mountain on which stands a castle of pearl [for he knew geography]. So I shall go into the desert and seek her there."

He went to the desert for many, many years. Then he saw

a huge man, a giant, of a size that was not human, who was carrying a huge tree, of a size that one does not see where men live. And the giant asked him, "Who are you?"

He answered, "I am a human being."

The giant was astonished and said, "I have been here in the desert for such a long time, and I have never yet seen a human being here."

The chamberlain told him the story of what had happened and how he was searching for a golden mountain on which stood a castle of pearl.

The giant answered, "There can be no such thing. It cannot be. People have been telling you stupid tales."

But the chamberlain insisted, "It must exist somewhere."

Then the giant said, "In my opinion, it is all nonsense, but since you insist, I shall help you. I am in charge of all the beasts. For your sake, I shall summon them all here. They run all over the world, and perhaps one of them knows about your mountain and castle."

So he summoned all the beasts, large and small, and questioned them. They all answered that they had not seen the mountain. He said, "You see, you have been told stupid tales. If you listen to me, you will turn back, because what you are seeking does not exist."

But the chamberlain insisted, "I know that it must exist."

Then the giant said, "I have a brother in the desert. He is in charge of all the birds. Perhaps they know, because they fly high in the air. Maybe they have seen the mountain and the castle. Go to him and tell him that I sent you." And the chamberlain went to search for him.

After many years he met a huge man, a giant who was also carrying a huge tree and who also questioned him, as the first one had. And the chamberlain told him the whole story, and that the giant's brother had sent him. And this giant, too, said that no such thing existed. But the chamberlain insisted that it must exist somewhere. Then the giant said, "I am in charge of all the birds, large and small. I shall summon them; perhaps they will know."

So he summoned all the birds, large and small, and questioned them. They all answered that they did not know of the mountain and the castle. He said, "You see, no such thing exists. If you listen to me, you will turn back because what you are seeking does not exist."

But the chamberlain persisted and said, "It certainly does exist, somewhere in the world."

The giant said, "Farther on in this same desert is my brother. He is in charge of the winds. Since they blow over the whole world, perhaps they will know."

And the chamberlain went on and searched for many years, and then he found another giant, who was also carrying a huge tree. The chamberlain told him also the story of what had happened. And this giant also tried to discourage him, telling him that no such thing existed. But the chamberlain persisted. So the giant said, "For your sake, I shall summon all the winds and question them."

So he summoned all the winds and asked them, and not one of them knew about the mountain and the castle. The giant said to the chamberlain, "You see, you have been told stupid tales."

Then the chamberlain began to weep and said, "I know that it does exist, somewhere in the world."

Meanwhile, the giant saw that another wind had come. He was angry with it and said, "Why are you late? Did I not summon all the winds? Why didn't you come with them?"

The wind answered, "I was delayed because I had to carry the daughter of a king to a golden mountain on which stands a castle of pearl."

The chamberlain was filled with joy. The giant asked the wind, "What precious things are in that place?"

The wind answered, "Everything there is precious."

Then the giant said to the chamberlain, "You have been searching for so long, and you have undergone many tribulations.

Perhaps lack of money is troubling you. I shall give you a vessel; when you put your hand into it, you will take out money." And he ordered the wind to take him to the mountain of gold.

So the storm wind came and carried him there and set him down by the gate of a city. Soldiers stood there and did not let him enter. So he put his hand in the vessel and took out money and bribed them, and he entered the city.

It was a beautiful city. And he went to a rich man and arranged to board with him, for he would have to spend time there; he would need to use wisdom and knowledge to get the king's daughter out.

And how he got her out of there, he did not relate.

But in the end he succeeded.

Commentary

The basic narrative of this story is not original. Versions that are similar in both general plot and particular details can be found in the Grimm brothers' tales and in Russian and Ukrainian folklore. Rabbi Nachman "adopted" this ancient folk tale, made a number of relatively small changes, and created a religious allegory of deep human significance. The transformation is so complete that in his introduction Nachman could write: "I told this story on the way, and everyone who heard it had thoughts of repentance."

In Nachman's rendering, the search for the king's daughter is symbolic of the quest to redeem the *Shekhinah* (God's presence in the world), which is held captive by the forces of evil. The king's chamberlain is symbolic of the people of Israel or, more specifically, of its spiritual leaders. The efforts to save the king's daughter, and the various failures are a tragic and poetic depiction of the historical struggle of the Jewish people—externally with the world and internally with its members.

THE LOSING OF THE KING'S DAUGHTER

In Nachman's stories where there is a king, he frequently represents the Supreme King, God Himself. This is clearly the case here, as it is also the case that the king's daughter is the *Shekhinah,* who is to a certain extent equivalent to *Knesset Israel,* the collective soul of Israel. The six sons also reflect certain details of the kabbalistic picture of the world. The special bond that exists between God and the *Shekhinah* (and *Knesset Israel*) is clearly established in the description of the king's affection for his daughter. This first passage recalls the time when the *Shekhinah* resided in the Temple in Jerusalem, and Israel lived in its land in close connection with God.

In an unexplained, and perhaps inexplicable, moment of crisis the king withholds his paternal care from his daughter, who is immediately snatched away by the powers of evil. The king immediately regrets what he has done and seeks to reestablish the original bond. Such a situation was in fact depicted by the prophet: "For a small moment have I forsaken thee; but with great compassion will I gather thee" (Isa. 54:7).

After the banishment of the *Shekhinah* the Jewish people, too, must go into exile. Here, in fact, Nachman has inverted the order of the traditional account in which the *Shekhinah* follows the Jews into exile—that is, the physical banishment precedes the spiritual. As Nachman tells it, the chamberlain makes a voluntary decision to seek out the king's daughter. Two tasks lie before him as leader of the people: to help the Jews find their collective soul, and to reunite daughter and father. To attain these goals, he is willing to suffer all the tribulations of an almost endless quest.

THE QUEST: STAGE I

When the chamberlain sets out, he takes with him no more than the basic necessities; in such a manner the Jewish people have had to leave their homes on numerous occasions. Nevertheless, he is accompanied by a servant, symbolic of the simple, innocent people of Israel who seek redemption together with their spiritual leaders, and who frequently have an important role to play. In two of Nachman's stories included in this book ("The Merchant and the Pauper" and "The Master of Prayer") the simple folk participate actively in the process, but here their role is secondary.

After years of searching, the chamberlain finds the king's daughter in the middle of the desert, which is traditionally the abode of the powers of evil (and also, paradoxically, where the divine revelation takes place and the Torah is given). The desert castle in which the daughter is held is described as if it were a regal palace; according to the symbolism of the story, this reflects the kabbalistic idea that the realm of evil resembles the actual world. Nevertheless, it is ultimately illusory. When the chamberlain overcomes his fear of the apparently powerful guards, he can enter unhampered. Evil is a mirror image of reality and has no power or even existence of its own. When man is aware of the nature of evil, he can enter its stronghold unharmed. The chamberlain penetrates the castle as an onlooker, and as such he sits in the corner.

The festivities in the kingdom of evil reach a climax when the queen—who is, of course, the king's daughter—is presented at court. Her regal status reflects the deeper level of significance of the exile of the *Shekhinah*: not only is she separated from the Divine, but she actually supports and sustains evil. The *Shekhinah* is, of course, not a willing partner, for she is a captive. The imagery used by the Kabbalah and Hasidism to describe the hold of evil on the *Shekhinah* is frequently powerful and dramatic.

The Baal Shem Tov, Nachman's great-grandfather, once said that the battle against evil is decided when one realizes that evil, too, contains something of the divine. This profound and difficult hasidic idea—which was frequently misunderstood—is central in this episode: the chamberlain recognizes the king's daughter in the midst of corruption, and at that moment the process of redemption is initiated. The next stage is her recognizing him and providing him with detailed instructions on how he is to rescue her. He is to perform certain tasks that are in fact spiritual exercises: penances, self-mortification, and incessant yearning.

The chamberlain's failure is almost inevitable. External evil can be overcome not by force but only by recognizing the Divine within it. Similarly, on the psychological level, the evil within man cannot be suppressed by asceticism and penances. The longer it is repressed, the more the evil inclination grows in strength. The problems that derive from strong natural desires must be resolved at their source, not at the level at which they are manifest. Though it is expressed in purely theological terms, this hasidic idea is similar to modern psychological theories.

The chamberlain's failure is reminiscent of the biblical account of the fall of Adam, who ate the forbidden fruit. Here the sin is followed by deep sleep, a decline, a kind of spiritual death in which there is no awareness or knowledge of the world. The Talmud describes sleep as being one sixtieth part of death. There is a surprising element here: the servant, who had no aspirations to achieve spiritual greatness, experiences no great fall and remains awake to look after the physical needs of the people.

THE QUEST: STAGE II

When the chamberlain finally awakens, he appears to have lost all sense of orientation and has to ask the servant what has happened. He returns to the king's daughter and finds her in the same place, for her exile is not yet total. His second task is easier—not to sleep when the great opportunity comes and not to drink wine, so as not to fall into a drunken slumber in which it would be impossible to distinguish between exile and redemption.

The task is easier; but the temptation, when it comes, is subtler, and the chamberlain succumbs to a species of formalistic reasoning. The commandment he received was quite clear, but he manages to find a casuistic way to circumvent it. Once again he falls into a deep sleep, this time for seventy years, the length of the Babylonian exile, during which, it is written, "We were as dreamers." This drunken slumber is so deep that all memory of the Redemption is lost. Indeed, not even the appeal of the king's daughter, the direct personal intervention of the *Shekhinah,* can arouse the chamberlain from his spiritual coma.

After this second failure the situation of the king's daughter is drastically changed and becomes symbolic of the final exile, when all hopes of immediate return are lost. She is banished to an inconceivably remote place. Nevertheless, she leaves the chamberlain a message, one that he can neither forget nor ignore. The Jewish people receive this letter, written in tears and suffering, which tells them that there is still hope, that the Redemption will come, but that it is far off and fantastic. Its beginning will be in a form and a place that are beyond human comprehension and experience—a golden mountain and a castle of pearl.

THE QUEST: THE FINAL STAGE

When Abraham was about to climb the mountain to sacrifice his son Isaac and was facing the most terrible test of faith imaginable, he told the servants who had accompanied him on the journey to stay behind. So, too, the chamberlain, about to go beyond the limits of human experience in search of the golden mountain, must go alone. The servant (the common people) endures the physical hardship of exile together with his master, but the latter must bear its spiritual torment and despair alone. This was the way that many hasidic leaders, and notably Nachman, envisaged their task: they had, on one hand, to direct and comfort their followers and, on the other, to face in isolation the spiritual challenges and existential loneliness of the final stages of the exile.

The final stage of the quest can be read at two levels, one geographical-historical, the other spiritual-metaphysical. Nachman frequently used the technique of ambiguous symbolism to present different messages within a single story to audiences of differing degrees of sophistication. At the first level, the quest goes deeper into exile through the centuries, and the giants are the various peoples among whom the Jewish people dwelled, who mocked their hopes and tested their faith. At the second level of significance, this last stage of the quest takes the chamberlain from the ordinary "real" world into another dimension of being, to other, metaphysical worlds. The golden mountain is not marked on any map of the world but exists in the higher spheres, and it is there that he must solve the problem of redemption. However, the exile of the *Shekhinah* is so deep and abysmal that not even the three giants, angels who rule over three such celestial worlds, can help. It is said that God did not reveal the time of the Redemption to any of his creatures, not even to the angels.

An interesting Jewish idea present in this episode is the status of man in relation to the angels. Man is small, a terrestrial being, whereas the angels are at a higher level in the cosmic scale. Nevertheless, the angels cannot move from their fixed positions, nor can they change their role. Man, on the other hand, is free in every meaning of the word.

The chamberlain has passed through many stages in his quest, from the first attempts to bring redemption by mortification of the body, to the spiritual voyages in which he encounters failure after failure. However, even after the third giant, the angel of the highest world he can reach, can help him no more and there is apparently no hope, his faith remains unbroken.

THE ROAD TO REDEMPTION

At this very point, the ultimate crisis of reality, many seekers after redemption gave up. In the rich vein of literature that deals with redemption, there are frequent descriptions of the time when the Messiah, son of Joseph (the precursor of the final Messiah, son of David), is killed, Jerusalem is destroyed again, and the few remaining believers flee into the wilderness. This is the moment of the greatest trial of faith, and those who pass it are the remnant who will see the Redemption.

Once again, good appears from within evil. The tidings that there is indeed a mountain of gold are brought by the very wind that transported the king's daughter to her place of exile; and the giant, who had previously declared that the search was futile, is willing to help, now that there are clear signs that the search can succeed.

The description of the chamberlain's entry into the city is brief, but it is replete with images drawn from messianic texts in the Talmud. The fact that the story does not end, and that the actual rescue of the king's daughter is not depicted, is typical of many of Nachman's stories and will be discussed again in later commentaries. At this point it is sufficient to note that the Redemption is a matter of the future, either remote or very close.

The Merchant and
the Pauper

ONCE there lived a merchant, a very rich man who possessed much wealth and many goods. His promissory notes reached every corner of the world. Everything that he desired was his. Nearby dwelt a pauper, a poor man who was in everything just the opposite of the merchant. Neither of them had children.

One night the merchant dreamed a dream: Several men came to his house and began to pack up all his possessions. He asked them what they were doing, and they replied that they were taking everything to the pauper who lived nearby. This answer provoked the merchant to great indignation, but since they were many and he was one, there was nothing he could do to stop them, and indeed they took everything in his house, leaving nothing but bare walls. He was naturally very upset, but when he woke up, he realized it had only been a dream, for, thank

God, his possessions were intact. Nevertheless, from that time on his heart was ill at ease, for he could not get the dream out of his mind.

Even before the dream the merchant used to look after and assist the pauper and his wife, but now he became even more concerned for their welfare. However, whenever the pauper or his wife came to his home, he recalled the dream and grew afraid, and his countenance changed. Moreover, both the pauper and his wife visited him frequently.

One day, the pauper's wife called on him. He gave her whatever she needed, but he was afraid, and his countenance changed. She asked him, "Your Honor, forgive me, but why is it that whenever I or my husband visit you, your countenance changes?" In reply, he told her about the dream and explained that this was why he became anxious every time he saw her or her husband. She asked whether the dream had been on such and such a night, giving a date.

"Yes," he answered, "but why do you ask?"

She replied, "On that very same night I too had a dream: I was very wealthy; several men came into my house and began to pack up all my possessions. I asked them what they were doing, and they told me they were taking everything to the pauper, that is to say, to the rich merchant who was now known as a pauper. So pay no attention to your dream. We all have our dreams."

However, after hearing this, the merchant became even more frightened and bewildered, for it seemed that something would really happen, that his wealth and possessions would go to the pauper, and that he would inherit the pauper's lot.

One day the merchant's wife went for a drive in a carriage. Among the female companions she took with her was the pauper's wife. A certain general happened to be traveling on the road at the time with a troop of soldiers; when he saw the carriage with its women travelers, he ordered that one of them be brought to him. The woman the soldiers chose was none other than the pauper's wife. They took her to the general's carriage and drove off with her.

There appeared to be no way to rescue her, since the general had many soldiers at his command, and he abducted her to his own country. However, she was an upright woman who feared God and would do no wrong; no matter how much they cajoled and implored her, she remained an upright, God-fearing woman. But she wept bitterly.

When the merchant's wife and her companions returned home from their drive without the pauper's wife, the unfortunate man was distraught. He wept incessantly and beat his head against the wall, bewailing the loss of his wife.

The merchant visited the pauper and asked him why he was weeping so bitterly. The pauper answered, "Why should I not weep? What is left to me? There are those who have wealth and others who have children, but I had only my wife. Now she has been taken from me. What is left to me?"

The merchant was deeply moved, and in the great compassion he felt for the poor man, he did something reckless, even mad. He found out where the general lived and set out to that country. There he performed a most extraordinary deed. He went directly to the general's fortified residence and, despite the guards that were posted all about, walked straight in. The guards were so startled by his impudence that they were incapable of action and did not stop him, and he, in turn, did not even look at them. He went into the general's quarters, straight to where the pauper's wife lay sleeping, woke her up, and said, "Come."

She was very frightened when she saw him, but he calmed her, telling her that she must leave with him immediately. Only when they had left, and had passed by all the guards on the way out, did he realize how reckless he had been. It was truly a rash deed, and there was certain to be a great outcry.

Shortly the alarm was raised, and together they hid for two days in a cistern full of rainwater, till the danger had passed. The pauper's wife was deeply moved by the great devotion the merchant was showing her and by the trials and tribulations he was enduring because of her, and she swore by God that whatever good fortune might in time be hers, she would deny him nothing. Whatever he desired of her future good fortune or prosperity, she would give him, even if by so doing she would become poor again. Now such an oath must be witnessed, and she made the very cistern in which they were hiding her witness.

Two days later they emerged and journeyed until they came to another place where, he realized, they were still being pursued. This time they found refuge in a bathing place. Once again she marked his devotion and the trials and tribulations he was enduring because of her, and once again she swore that if fortune ever favored her, she would deny him nothing. This time she called upon the reservoir as her witness. They remained there, too, for about two days, and then they continued on their journey. When the merchant discovered that their pursuers had once more caught up with them, they hid again. This happened seven times. Seven times they were in danger, and seven times they concealed themselves by water: in a cistern, in a bathing place, by a lake, a spring, a creek, a river, and a sea; and in each place of concealment she noted his devotion and the trials and tribulations he was enduring because of her, and she swore her oath and called on the place itself as a witness. This happened seven times, until they came to the sea.

The merchant was a great trader and knew the routes across the sea, and so they returned quickly to their own country, where he restored the pauper's wife to her husband. Thereupon there was a great rejoicing.

In reward for his extraordinary deed and for his having withstood temptation with another man's wife, God gave the merchant a son, born that very year. The pauper's wife, too, was rewarded for having withstood temptation with the general and with the merchant, and gave birth to a daughter. This girl was extremely beautiful. Her beauty was sublime, unlike that found among mortals, and people used to say, "May she be spared," for such a phenomenal child is raised with difficulty.

Such beauty and splendor had never been seen by man before. People used to come from afar just to look upon her and showered many gifts of affection upon her. These gifts were so numerous that before long the pauper became rich.

It occurred to the merchant that he should arrange a match between his son and the pauper's daughter, because of her great and unique beauty. This, he thought, might be the significance of the dreams in which all his possessions were transferred to the pauper and those of the pauper to him; were the children joined in marriage, the two families would be united.

One day the pauper's wife came to visit the merchant, and he told her of his desire to arrange a match and thereby, perhaps, fulfill their dreams. She answered, "I too have considered this, but I did not dare to raise the subject. If, however, it is your desire too, I am certainly willing. I shall deny you nothing. Have I not sworn that all my good fortune will always be at your disposal?"

The son and the daughter studied together, learning languages and arts and sciences. The daughter's beauty continued to grow. People continued to visit her just to look upon her beauty, and the gifts they brought made the pauper a very rich man. Even the nobility came to see her, and in their eyes, too, her beauty was unique. It was no mortal loveliness. These nobles began to consider the possibility of arranging a match with the pauper, and there was one in particular who wished to pledge his son to the beautiful daughter. However, nobility cannot intermarry with common folk, and so they sought to raise the pauper's status by arranging for him to go into service with the emperor.

At first he was a sergeant, but he was rapidly promoted. So many noblemen were interested in his advancement that he rose swiftly through the ranks. All wished to make a match with him, and all sought his promotion. Nevertheless, as his daughter was engaged to another, he could not conclude a match, and the matter was left conveniently open. Eventually he became a general. He succeeded so well that the emperor sent him to fight wars, and he was victorious every time. He became a very high and mighty person. When the emperor died, the councils of the people assembled and proposed him as the new ruler, whereupon the nobles convened and appointed him emperor. The new emperor went on to fight many wars and conquer many lands. After a while other countries came to hear of his great success. They began to surrender to him voluntarily because all the beauty and all the good fortune in the world appeared to be with him. Eventually all the kings in the world convened and decided that he should rule over them. They made him emperor over the whole world, and they gave him a document inscribed with letters of gold.

The emperor was no longer willing to keep to the promise of a marriage bond with the merchant's family. Is it fitting that an emperor should give his daughter to the son of a merchant? On the other hand, his wife, now empress, refused to withdraw from the agreement. When the emperor saw that he would not be able to arrange an alternative match for his daughter as long as the merchant stood in his path, all the more so since his wife remained loyal, he began to devise means of getting rid of him. First he intrigued by plot and deceit to impoverish him; it was not difficult for the emperor to do this and, shortly the merchant started to lose money and become a pauper. Even so, the empress remained steadfast in her pledge.

The emperor then realized that he would not be able to make another match for his daughter as long as the merchant's son was alive, and he devised means to dispose of him. He had the young man brought to trial and told the judges what verdict and sentence he wanted. The merchant's son was accordingly condemned to be tied up in a sack and cast into the sea.

The empress was deeply grieved, but she was powerless to act against the emperor. So she went to the officials whose task it was to carry out the sentence and fell at their feet and implored them for her sake to spare the young man. What had he done to deserve death? She begged them to let the innocent young man go free and to cast some other condemned prisoner, who truly deserved such a fate, into the sea in his place. Her pleading was successful, and they swore to her that they would do as she asked. Accordingly, they cast someone else into the sea and released the young man, telling him to make his escape immediately. And so the merchant's son, now grown up, went into exile.

Even before this had happened, the empress had told her daughter that the merchant's son was her appointed bridegroom. The mother told her daughter the whole story of what had befallen her, of how the merchant had shown such devotion and had endured hardships and danger for her sake. "He was with me in seven places of concealment, and in each of them I swore by God that I would never withhold from him anything that belonged to me. I called on each of these seven places of water as a witness. You are now all my success and my good fortune, and it is clear that you are his, and he is yours. However, your father has been blinded by pride and seeks to have the young man killed. Even so, my daughter, you must always remember that he is your appointed bridegroom and never agree to another in his place."

The daughter was a God-fearing person, and she took her mother's words to heart, promising to honor the pledge. She sent the merchant's son a letter to the effect that she regarded herself as betrothed to him and him alone as her bridegroom. She also sent him a map that she had drawn, showing all the places in which her mother had hidden with his father, the seven witnesses to her mother's oath, the cistern, the reservoir, and the others. She charged him to take great care of this document, which she signed with her name.

After the merchant's son had been set free by those appointed to put him to death, he set out on his travels. After some time he reached the sea and set sail. A tempest arose and drove his ship onto a desert coast, where it was wrecked. However, all the passengers were saved and went ashore. As the coast was remote from all shipping routes, so that no help could be expected from the sea, the survivors separated, each one making his own way in search of food and water.

The young man also set out into the wilderness; he walked farther and farther from the shore, until he could no longer return. The more he tried to find his way back, the deeper he wandered into the wilderness, until he realized there was no return. He had a bow and arrow with which he defended himself against the wild beasts of the wilderness, and he found sufficient food. Eventually he emerged from the desert and he reached a place that was habitable, but in which no one lived. Water was there in abundance, and trees that bore fruit. He decided to settle there, for it would be difficult to return to civilization. Since there was fruit to eat and water to drink, and he could shoot an occasional hare or deer with his bow for meat and even catch delicious fish in the stream, it seemed an excellent place to spend the rest of his life.

The emperor, believing that the sentence had been carried out and that the merchant's son was no longer alive, felt he could now proceed to arrange a suitable match for his daughter, and negotiations began with various kings. He built a suitable royal court for her, and she lived there with the nobles' daughters she had chosen to be her companions. She spent her time playing various musical instruments, rejecting all ideas of a ne-

gotiated match, and insisting that each and every suitor come
to her in person.

The emperor's daughter was very proficient in the art of
poetry. A special podium was constructed on which the royal
suitors stood when they declaimed their poems of love and
desire, each one with his words of love. To some she sent an
answer, also in verse and in words of affection, through one of
her noble companions. To others, who pleased her more, she
herself declaimed the verses of her affectionate reply. And to
those who pleased her more, she showed herself and let them
look upon her face when she answered. However, she rejected
them all, ending her answer with the words that none understood: "But the waters have not passed over you. . . ." The
suitors to whom she revealed her face were overwhelmed by her
beauty: some would swoon, whereas others went mad with love.
Kings continued to seek her hand, and nevertheless to all of
them she gave the same reply.

The merchant's son settled down in his deserted spot. He,
too, was proficient in verse and learned in the art of music. He
found suitable wood and fashioned musical instruments and
made strings from animal gut, and he played and sang to
himself. Occasionally he would take out the letter from the
emperor's daughter and play and sing, recalling everything
that had befallen him from the time that his father had been a
rich merchant to his exile in this place.

One day he went into the forest, selected a tree, and made
a mark on it. Then he carved out a hollow and hid the letter in
it and stayed there for a while. Sometime later a great tempest
felled all the trees in the forest, and he could no longer find
the one in which he had hidden the letter. When the forest had
been intact, he could recognize his own tree by the mark he had
made; but now that it was one among a fallen, broken multitude,
this was no longer possible. It was not feasible to split open all
the trees in order to find the letter, for there were too many.

He was grief-stricken and wept greatly. He realized that were he to remain there, he would go mad with regret and sorrow, and so he decided to leave. No matter what might happen to him on the way, it would be more dangerous for him to dwell there in his grief.

He packed some meat and fruit in his knapsack and set out on his way, making marks to show him the way back.

After a while he reached a town, and he asked in which country he was. The people told him, and he asked if they knew anything about the emperor. They said that they did. Then he inquired about the emperor's beautiful daughter, and they replied that they had heard about her, and that no suitor could win her hand in marriage.

Since he could not go to her in person, he approached the king of that country and told him the whole story: that he was the true bridegroom of the emperor's daughter, and that this was the reason for her refusing to marry anyone else. Since he himself could not go near the emperor's court, he would give the king certain signs, like the seven places of water, that the king might go and arrange the marriage with her, for which he would be properly compensated. The king recognized that the young man was speaking the truth, for such a story could hardly be contrived, and so he accepted the mission. However, he realized that it would not be to his benefit to bring the daughter back with the young man still there. On the other hand, he was not inclined to have him killed, for, after all, the young man had done him a favor. So the king decided to exile him to another land, about two hundred miles distant.

The young man was very vexed that he had been banished just because of the good deed he had done for the king, so he went to the king of the second country, and to him, too, he told the entire story, giving him the signs—but in greater detail—and urging him to set out immediately in order to reach the emperor's daughter before the first king. Even were he to get there after the first, his signs would be more convincing. However, this second king thought like the first, and he, too, exiled the young man to a land two hundred miles away.

The merchant's son was very vexed, and he approached a third king, to whom he gave even more signs and proofs, including instructions on how to draw the map of the seven places of concealment. But this king, too, thought like the others and sent the young man two hundred miles away. Meanwhile, the first king traveled quickly and called on the emperor's daughter. He composed a poem, skillfully introducing in it all the places of water, that is, the seven witnesses to the mother's oath. However, he arranged the names as they sounded best to him, according to the rules of poetry, rather than in the correct order. The emperor's daughter was astonished to hear the seven secret places mentioned, and she thought that he was indeed her bridegroom. He had indeed failed to mention the places in their proper order, and that caused her some difficulty, but she thought that it could probably be attributed to the requirements of art and prosody, so she decided that he was the one. She wrote him a note saying that she accepted his suit. There was much rejoicing and excitement at the news that the beautiful daughter had found herself a groom, and preparations were begun for the wedding.

Meanwhile, the second king, who had been given even more signs by the merchant's son, made haste and arrived at the royal residence. When he was told that she had already chosen a bridegroom, he paid no attention, saying that he had something to say that would certainly succeed. They let him present his suit, and in his poem he gave all the places in the proper order and, furthermore, added one more sign. She asked him how the first king, too, had known the signs; but since he could not tell the truth, he said he did not know. All this was most strange to her, and she wondered how the first king had known the places that no man could possibly guess. Nevertheless, she decided that the second king must be her bridegroom, since he had given the places in the correct order with an additional sign. She thought that the first king had probably uttered the places as poetic fancy without knowing what they meant.

Meanwhile, the third king, who had been given even more convincing signs and also had a map, made haste and presented himself as a prospective groom. He, too, was told that she had already made her choice, but he said he had something that would certainly succeed. And so the third king entered and recited his poem with its even more convincing signs and then showed her the copy of the map. She was now completely bewildered and at a loss. The first and second kings had also mentioned the places, and she therefore declared that she would believe no one who did not bring her own letter.

The merchant's son grew weary of being sent away time after time and decided to present himself before the emperor's daughter; perhaps he would succeed by himself. When at last he arrived, he told her companions that he had something to tell her that would certainly succeed. They let him in too, and he recited his poem. The signs he cited were even more convincing than those of the others, and in addition he reminded her of their youth and how they had studied together in the same class. He told her how in fact he himself had sent the three kings after he had lost the original letter in the tree, but she was so confused that she refused to heed what he said; after all, the other kings had also made excuses about why they did not have the original letter, and after many years she could not possibly recognize him. In fact she decided not to rely on the signs; from now on she would accept only her own letter.

Realizing that he could do nothing to convince her, the merchant's son decided to return to his place in the wilderness and to spend the rest of his life there. He was dismayed by the people in the world and thought that it was better to live out his remaining years in solitude. So he wandered around for several years until he found his way back to his place in the desert and settled there, eating the fruit of the trees, as before.

Now there was a murderous scoundrel who lived on the sea. When this murderer heard of the existence of the wondrous beauty, he sought to capture her; he did not want her for himself, being a eunuch, but thought that he would be able to sell her to a king for a large sum of money. He was an unprincipled scoundrel and, like all murderers, quite unconcerned about what would happen to him if he failed. He began to take the necessary steps to implement his scheme. First he bought a huge amount of goods of magnificent quality and variety; then he made birds of gold, so artfully contrived they seemed actually to be alive, and prepared stalks of gold as perches. Such large birds standing on thin stalks which did not break appeared to be a great wonder. In addition, he contrived to make it appear that they were singing, one clucking with its beak, another whistling, and another trilling. It was in fact all a clever trick; concealed actors made the appropriate sounds, and the birds were moved by strings.

Then the murderer set sail with his cargo. When he reached the land where the emperor's daughter resided, he dropped anchor and presented himself as a great merchant with many goods to sell. People came on board his ship to buy many kinds of precious objects. He remained there for some time, three months or more, and all the while the townsfolk came to buy from him, and they showed what they had purchased to others.

The emperor's daughter also desired to purchase something, so she sent him a note, inviting him to bring her some of his goods. He replied that it was not his practice to bring merchandise to the buyer, and anyone who wished to purchase from him, even an emperor's daughter, would have to come to him. Nobody could force him to act otherwise. The emperor's daughter decided to go to him. As was her custom on leaving the palace, she veiled her face, lest anyone who saw her beauty be smitten by it and fall in a swoon. Together with some of her companions and a guard, she visited the merchant, who was none other than the murderous scoundrel, and purchased various objects. When they departed, the merchant told her that if she came again, he would show her even more beautiful objects, wonderful and rare.

She visited the merchant again, buying things. After a while she became a regular visitor to the ship. One day he opened the special chamber where the golden birds were standing, and when she saw them she was overcome with amazement. The soldiers and her companions also wanted to look, but he refused to let them, telling her, "No, no. I won't show them to anybody but you, for you are the emperor's daughter." So she went in by herself, but he followed her, locked the door, overpowered her, and put her into a sack. Then he stripped off her clothes and gave them to a sailor to wear, also making him veil his face; he pushed the sailor out and told him to leave. This sailor had no idea what was happening and walked off the ship; the soldiers and companions who were waiting for the emperor's daughter joined him, and he followed them to the palace. Here his face was unveiled, and there was great commotion and furor. The sailor was flogged, but as it was clear that he knew nothing and was not guilty, they threw him out.

The murderer, knowing well that they would be pursued, left the ship with the emperor's daughter and hid together with her in a cistern until the danger had passed. Beforehand he had charged the sailors on the ship to raise anchor and set sail immediately, reassuring them that the pursuers would not shoot at a ship in which they thought the emperor's daughter was held captive. Actually, he did not care if the ship was intercepted. Like all reckless scoundrels, he was indifferent to what befell him or anyone else.

And so it was. The alarm was raised, and pursuit was given. The ship was caught, but of course the emperor's daughter was not on it. Hiding with her in the cistern, the murderer warned her to make no noise or call for help: "I have risked my life to capture you. If I lose you, my life will be worth nothing. So I have no scruples, and if you make the slightest sound, I shall strangle you at once. Come what may, I know how little I am worth, and I don't care what happens to me."

The emperor's daughter was mortally afraid and kept silent. When they left the cistern, they roamed in the city until once more they were in danger of being discovered, whereupon they hid in another place of water, a bathing place. This was repeated seven times, in the very same seven kinds of places of concealment in which the merchant had once hidden with her mother. They were the places of water that were witnesses to her mother's oath: a cistern, a bathing place, a lake, a spring, a creek, and a river; and eventually they came to the sea. There he found a small fishing vessel and set sail with her. He did not desire her for himself, being a eunuch, but he wished to sell her to a king. Fearing that she would be recognized, he dressed her as a sailor, so that she looked like a man.

Thus they crossed the sea. A tempest arose and tossed the fishing vessel onto the shore, breaking it up completely. Now the shore was none other than the desert land upon which the young man had once been shipwrecked and where he had found himself a place to live.

The murderer, who was acquainted with shipping routes, knew that no vessels visited that shore; he thus knew that there was no danger of discovery, and he let her walk by herself. They each went in search of food, and the emperor's daughter managed to elude him. As soon as the scoundrel realized that she was out of sight, he began to shout. She did not answer, realizing that there was no need. Were he to discover her, she could always pretend that she had not heard him. As his aim was to sell her, he would have nothing to gain by killing her. So she kept quiet and eluded him. The murderer searched for her in vain, and eventually he was devoured by wild beasts.

She wandered on, finding food on the way. After a while she reached the place where the young man, the merchant's son, had settled. She was unkempt and dressed like a sailor, and they did not recognize each other; still he was very happy to have someone to talk to.

He asked the apparent sailor, "How did you get here?"

She answered, "I was with a merchant at sea and we were shipwrecked."

He told her that he, too, had been with a merchant at sea and had been shipwrecked.

And the two of them lived there together.

The empress was grief-stricken by her daughter's abduction. She beat her head against the wall and blamed her husband, the emperor, saying that because of his pride he had killed the young man, and now he had lost their daughter. She wept, saying that their daughter had been all their good fortune and prosperity, and now she was gone. "What is left to me?" she moaned. The emperor was already grieved at the loss of his daughter, and her accusations added much to the anger and strife between them. He grew so furious that he decided to get rid of her. Accordingly, he arranged for a court of justice to banish her.

When the emperor next sent his armies to war, they failed him. He placed the blame on the general, saying the war had been lost because of his mistakes. The general was banished. Then once again he sent his armies, and once again they failed, and yet another general was banished. In this way several generals were dismissed. The citizens soon realized that strange things were happening, that the emperor had banished first the empress and then all the generals, and they thought that perhaps it should have been the other way around. Accordingly, they banished the emperor and restored the empress and the generals. The empress's first act as a ruler was to send for the merchant and his wife and have them brought to live in the palace.

When the emperor was dismissed, he pleaded to be given his liberty. "I have been your emperor, and I have done many good things. So have mercy on me, and let me be free to move about in my exile. I shall never return, and you need have no fear of me. Let me go and live the rest of my days in peace."

So the emperor, too, went into exile; at long last he reached the sea and set sail. A tempest arose and cast him onto the very same shore upon which his daughter had been shipwrecked. He walked through the desert until he reached the place where the merchant's son and his own beautiful daughter, now dressed as a sailor, were living together. They did not recognize each other, for several years had elapsed, and their hair, too, had grown long and wild. They asked him how he had come there, and he told them that he had been traveling with a merchant and had been shipwrecked. They told him that that was how they, too, had come to be there.

Thus the three of them lived there together, eating of the fruit of the trees and drinking from the stream. They made music, for each was able to play instruments. The young man was the strongest and most capable, for he had been there longest, so he hunted and brought them meat. They burned wood which in towns is more precious than gold. The young man sought to prove that this was the best place to spend the rest of their days, in this wilderness. It was a much better life than that pursued in towns and cities, he said. They asked him what kind of life he had led before coming here that enabled him to state that this life was better. He told them that he had been the son of a rich merchant and had had everything that he desired, but here, too, he had everything he wanted; and he continued to prevail upon them to spend the rest of their lives where they were.

The emperor asked him whether he had heard about the emperor, to which the young man replied that he had. Then the emperor asked whether he had heard about the emperor's beautiful daughter; this time, too, the young man replied that he had. He became very angry, declaring that the emperor was a murderer. (He did not know of course that he was speaking to the emperor himself.) The emperor asked why, and the young man said that he was there because of the emperor's cruelty and pride. The emperor asked how this was so, and since the young man had nothing to fear, he told the whole story of what had befallen him. (Previously he had said only that he was a merchant's son.)

The emperor asked him, "Were the emperor to fall into your hands now, would you take your revenge on him?"

"No," he answered, for he was a merciful man. "On the contrary, I would look after him just as I am taking care of you."

The emperor then began to bemoan all the evil and bitterness that had befallen this emperor. For he had heard, so he said, that his beautiful daughter had been abducted and he himself banished.

The merchant's son said that it was because of the emperor's cruelty and pride that he had lost his daughter and been banished himself, and that for the same reason he, the young man, had found his way here. It was all the emperor's own fault.

Whereupon the emperor asked him again, "Were that emperor here, would you revenge yourself on him?"

And again the young man answered that he would not: "I would look after him just as I am taking care of you."

Then the emperor revealed that he was himself none other than the emperor, and he told him everything that had befallen him.

The young man took him in his arms, embraced him, and kissed him, while the beautiful daughter, who was disguised as a sailor, looked on and listened to all that passed between them.

The Merchant and the Pauper

Every day the young man was wont to go out to the forest to search for the hidden letter. There were thousands upon thousands of trees, and each day he went out and cut a mark on the three trees in which he had searched that day. When he returned, his eyes were always tearful from weeping. They asked him what he was seeking that brought him back with tearful eyes, and he told them the entire story of the letter the emperor's daughter had sent him, of how he had hidden it in a tree for safekeeping and how the tempest had utterly changed the appearance of the forest. He was still searching for the letter and still hoped to find it. Then they said to him, "Tomorrow we will come to search with you. Perhaps we will be successful."

So they began to accompany him to the forest, and each of them searched among the trees, until one day the emperor's daughter found the letter. She saw that it was indeed the letter she had sent him, in her own handwriting. However, she felt that it would be dangerous were she to reveal everything at once. Were she suddenly to disclose her identity, remove her disguise, and reappear in her former beauty, the shock would be too much for the young man, and he might faint or die. Furthermore, she wanted to be married properly, so they could not stay in the wilderness. So she gave him the letter, merely telling him where she had found it. He fainted, but they revived him, and there was much rejoicing among them.

Afterward, however, the young man said, "What do I need the letter for now? Where can I find her? She is certainly with some king by now. What do I need it all for anyway? I shall spend the rest of my life here." So he returned the letter to her, saying, "Here, you take the letter, find her, and marry her." (For she was dressed as a man.)

She let herself be persuaded but begged him to accompany her, saying, "I shall surely find her, and it will go well with me. But I should like to share my good fortune with you."

The young man saw that she, whom he thought to be a

sailor, was very clever and was sure to win the emperor's daughter, so he was pleased to accompany him—that is, the emperor's daughter.

The emperor wanted to remain there alone, for he was afraid to return to that land over which he had once ruled, but the sailor—that is, his daughter—persuaded him to come along too. Were he to win the beautiful maiden, there would be nothing to fear: the wheel of fortune would be reversed, and the emperor restored.

So the three of them set out and hired a ship. They crossed the sea and came to the land where the empress ruled. As they approached the city, the daughter thought that were she to reveal herself to her mother too suddenly, the shock would be too much. So she first sent the empress a message that someone had arrived with information about her daughter. Then the daughter went in person and told the empress everything that had befallen her daughter. At the end the daughter said, "And she is here." Then she told the truth: "It is I. . . . I am your daughter." She also told her mother that her bridegroom, the merchant's son, was there too. In addition, she said that she wanted her father restored to his country. At first her mother would not hear of it, as she was still angry at him for having been the cause of all the trouble, but for her daughter's sake she agreed; first, however, it would be necessary to find him, and nobody knew where he was. Then the daughter said, "He, too, is here, together with us."

Then the merchant's son and the beautiful daughter were wed, and the happiness was complete. The new couple received the kingdom and the empire, and they ruled over the whole world. Amen.

Commentary

The plot of "The Merchant and the Pauper" is largely an original creation, though certain folk elements from various sources have been skillfully woven into the narrative. In its literary form and structure it is more polished than the preceding tale. A single narrative line runs from beginning to end, and subthemes flow smoothly into the development of the main plot.

"The Merchant and the Pauper" is one of Nachman's heavily allegorical stories. As in "The Losing of the King's Daughter," the basic theme is the Redemption and the processes that lead up to it, but here greater emphasis is placed on the personality of the Messiah. The major theological issues that underlie the story concern the relationships between the Jewish people as a whole (*Knesset Israel,* the collective soul of Israel identified with the *Shekhinah*) and the first and the final redeemers.

The merchant and the pauper, the first two characters to be introduced, represent specific historical personalities, but they are also an essential part of the symbolic fabric of the story. The merchant is the whole man whose wealth is both worldly and spiritual, while the pauper is the man who remains poor in spirit, even after he has attained material success; the one is noble, possessing an abundance of spiritual values, and the other, a simple man of the people. The dreams of the merchant and the pauper's wife and their fulfillment fit into this typology and reflect a hasidic notion that in certain generations the base are raised up both materially and spiritually, while the spiritually great are cast down. The pauper's wife embodies the positive aspects of the poor—modesty, innocence, and loyalty to values and relationships in changing circumstances. On the allegorical level, she represents the simple people of Israel, and the adventures that befall her echo the events of Jewish history. At the beginning of the story she is abducted by the general; this is the first captivity, the exile in Egypt. The merchant (who represents the historical Moses) feels obliged to save the woman —that is, the children of Israel. The historical mission—to enable a whole people to slip out of Egypt—appeared to be impractical and beyond human capabilities; indeed, it was conceived and executed almost recklessly, with no real weighing of alternatives or planning for contingencies in the desert. It came about as the result of an individual's irrepressible impulse rather than by popular demand.

Emergence from exile is fraught not only with physical danger but also with spiritual perils, such as the temptation to return to the fleshpots of Egypt and repeat the incident of the golden calf; the Exodus must therefore proceed by a long, circuitous route. It is a vast drama that involves, on the human level, stages of purification and increasing commitment and, on the divine level, revelation and concealment. In the biblical account of the Exodus, the children of Israel go from one watering place to another and make seven different passages of water (from the Red Sea to the Jordan), at each of which an event renews the bond and covenant between savior and saved. In the symbolism of the Kabbalah, each station represents one of the seven lower *Sefirot,* and the water itself is the divine plenty. In Nachman's story, the Exodus is retold in allegory, and the seven pledges made by the pauper's wife to remember the rescue are symbolic both of the eternal covenant between Israel and God and of the bond between redeemer and redeemed.

The children born to the two couples are the central characters in the allegory, and their significance is to be understood in terms of the Kabbalah. The pauper's daughter is *Knesset Israel,* the *Shekhinah,* the presence of God in the world. Whereas the mother is Israel as seen in her simplicity and poverty, the daughter is the glory of Israel, the symbol of all that the *Shekhinah* can bestow on humanity. The merchant's son is clearly the Messiah. This connection between Moses and the Messiah, the first and the final redeemers, is ancient and well established in many Jewish sources.

There are thus two aspects, two manifestations, of Israel: the lowly pauper's wife and her beautiful daughter. The *Shekhinah* is the source of all life, and all men wish to enjoy her beauty. At her advent in the world, she is adored by and enthralls all mankind, Jews and gentiles alike; everyone wishes to participate in the wondrous revelation. Paradoxically at this critical stage of history it is not the person of noble spirit, the merchant, who is raised up, but the poor and simple man, the father of the *Shekhinah*. The merchant is given no post in this new state of affairs, and consequently he loses his wealth, while his son— the future Messiah—is perceived as a threat by the new emperor. This ignoble character achieves worldly power and glory by means of the divine splendor of his daughter. Having attained external wealth, the pauper loses interest in true salvation and tries to discourage contact between *Knesset Israel* and the Messiah; sovereignty over the physical world is enough for him.

The pauper's wife, as I have noted, represents another side of the simple person. Even as the highly placed wife of the emperor, she retains her innocence and remains loyal to her pledge to the first savior; furthermore, she makes her daughter a party to it by having her promise to be faithful to the merchant's son, the future savior. The pledge the daughter grants him, the sign by which she will recognize him, is the memory of the first salvation; the final salvation reflects and completes the first. The merchant's son possesses the only copy of this written pledge, which is not the folk memory of the Exodus but rather an esoteric, encoded document, and thus he alone can learn the secrets of her soul and the means to bring about her redemption.

The concept of the exiled Messiah is known in many Jewish

sources, but in the form in which it is retold here, many of the details have clear kabbalistic connotations: the storm that carries the Messiah off is a symbol of the forces of evil, and the place of his refuge reflects the kabbalistic idea that the soul of the Messiah resides in the Garden of Eden until the time comes for him to appear.

The theme of the many suitors wooing the apparently abandoned princess is a relic of numerous folk tales, but here it is invested with symbolic significance and associations. The great men of all generations have sought to approach the *Shekhinah*, but with limited success. Some suitors are denied permission even to enter into her presence; others, in language reminiscent of a famous talmudic text dealing with mystic knowledge, enter, gaze upon her, but are stricken with madness; even those who are worthy of looking upon the divine presence soon proceed no further, for they have not reached the stature of the Messiah.

The merchant's son is reluctant to leave the Garden of Eden unless he is certain that he will be able to find the beautiful daughter. His reluctance must be overcome. Paradoxically it is the forces of evil, the storm, that uproot the trees of Eden, thereby activating him and initiating the beginning of the redemption. The precious pledge is lost, and he has to try to redeem the princess without it. However, he is forced to reveal part of his secret, though not the actual pledge, to certain people who usurp his trust and present themselves as the daughter's betrothed.

This episode is an allegorical account of the various messianic figures who have crossed the stage of Jewish history, frequently with disastrous results. Possessing part of the secret signs and perhaps some aspect of messiahship, each was able for a time to persuade the people, including the leaders, that he was indeed the redeemer. (A famous example is that of the sage Rabbi Akiva, who was convinced that Bar Kochba, leader of the revolt against the Romans in 135 C.E., was the Messiah-king.) Each of the personalities in the story was requested to help in bringing about the redemption, but instead each attempted to usurp the redeemer's role for himself. In a tantalizing detail, Nachman seems to imply that the true Messiah has indeed come once, only to be rejected. To whom was he referring? Who among the false messiahs was the true one? The moral of this section is clear: neither charismatic personality nor partially fulfilled prophecies are acceptable as proof of the Messiah's identity; only unequivocal, documentary evidence will serve.

According to much Jewish thought, especially as developed in the Kabbalah, the Redemption will come not as the result of a single act or move of the Messiah but through a dialectic process in which the *Shekhinah, Knesset Israel*—in this story, the daughter—must seek him out; the daughter, as it were, must activate her redeemer. In the first stage she must pass through suffering, oppression, and exile. Though the tribulations she must endure reflect to a certain degree those of her mother, their content and purpose are entirely different. The mother's route is through purification and commitment, while the daughter is drawn into degradation and isolation; this is what the Kabbalah describes as the "descent necessary for the ultimate ascent," a dialectic that describes both cosmic processes and the cycles of the human soul.

The scoundrel who carries the daughter off is a personification of evil; not only is he a murderer, but he also makes a living from death and thus can be identified with Satan in his role as the Angel of Death. One of the characteristics of evil is that it has no creative power, and thus the scoundrel is a eunuch. He desires the daughter not for love or even lust, but in order to exploit her beauty by selling her for a high price. Evil is essentially parasitic.

The technique by which the scoundrel lures the daughter into his cabin is typical of the way evil tempts man: beginning with trifles, transactions of little significance, it draws man on through better bargains to the promised ultimate marvel, which is in fact an illusion and a fraud. But by the time this is discovered, it is too late to turn back.

At the beginning of her exile, the daughter is stripped of her magnificent garments, her outer manifestations, and is wrapped in a sack, mark of the lowest level of being. Furthermore, the scoundrel fashions a substitute: instead of the *Shekhinah* in her glory, he takes a sailor, a role lacking ultimate significance, and clothes him in her garments. It is the nature of evil to extract the inner content and to replace it with a void, thereby creating a false mystery. This spurious manifestation of holiness can be successful only temporarily, but still long enough for the servants to be decoyed and the scoundrel to make his escape. The sailor is clearly not the author of the deception and is set free with only token reproof.

Paradoxically, when the scoundrel finally reaches what would seem to be his true environment, the wilderness, he is defeated, and the process of redemption, of ascent, begins. The daughter has reached the depths of her degradation: she can descend no more, and thus evil can no longer exert power over her. The scoundrel is essentially a parasite, and once separated from her, he loses the source of his life. Evil draws all its sustenance by attaching itself to holiness and, if severed from it, perishes. Thus, when the scoundrel is left alone, the wild beasts devour him.

The role of the daughter is no longer passive. She becomes an active agent in the process of redemption and now must take the initiative. In the symbolism of the story this transformation in her nature is reflected in her being dressed in the garments of a man. However, even her eventual discovery of the merchant's son in the Garden of Eden cannot bring about the Redemption. Until the corruption and disharmony in the world order have been put right, she cannot reveal herself to him.

The emperor is spiritually obtuse and never realizes that the beauty of his daughter is the source of his power. When she is lost and his fortunes decline, he typically blames and punishes others for his failures. Finally he, too, is banished and makes his way to the wilderness for the denouement. He now hands sovereignty over to his wife, the empress. An essential component of the process of redemption is action from below, the contribution of the common folk.

The savior appears to have despaired of his task of salvation and to have relinquished hope of changing the outer world: for him will suffice a life of wholeness and simplicity (in which he can burn "wood which in towns is more precious than gold"). He even tries to persuade his companions to accept this life in the wilderness, this undefined dream world where there is, indeed, no salvation, but neither is there the tribulation of exile. This lack of interest in personal success and achievement is apparently a necessary stage in his development. He is, however, not entirely passive, and when in due course the identity of the banished emperor is revealed, he effects a reconciliation. This is necessary, because even though the emperor no longer wields power, he still has a role to play in the life of his daughter and, indeed, of the people. The Messiah continues his search for the document that is the key to salvation. Ultimately, though, it is not he but the daughter who finds it, and it is also she who makes all the active preparations for the Redemption. The alienation of exile comes to an end, and the divine plan for human existence is implemented. Nachman thus demonstrates that a number of factors are involved in the process of redemption. It is not enough to wait passively for the Messiah, for he is in fact inactive at certain critical stages.

The conclusion of the story, the happy end, is symbolic of the restitution of order and harmony at all levels of the reestablishment of eternal values. The major role in bringing this about is played by the *Shekhinah, Knesset Israel*. However, the contribution of the common folk, the life and deeds of each individual Jew, is an essential factor.

The King's Son and the Son of the Maid

ONCE there was a king. In his household there was a certain maid who served the queen. She was not a simple cook who would never be allowed in the king's presence, but a maid-in-waiting of modest rank.

When the time came for the queen to deliver her child, the maid too was ready to give birth. The midwife, for no other reason than to see what would come of it, exchanged the babies. She took the king's son and laid it next to the maid, and she laid the maid's son next to the queen.

The boys began to grow up. The so-called son of the king, who was really the son of the servant, was given much honor and respect. He was raised up higher and higher and became greatly exalted. Meanwhile, the maid's son—that is, the king's true son—grew up in the king's household, and both children studied together in the same class. The king's true son was by nature drawn to regal ways, even though he was brought up in the home of a servant. Conversely, the maid's son, who was known as the king's son, was drawn to ways that were not those of a king, but as he was brought up in the house of the king, he had to behave according to the regal manners which he had been taught.

Now women are incapable of keeping a secret, and after a while the midwife told someone how she had exchanged the two infants. As this man had a friend, and this friend also had a friend, the secret naturally became known, and before long everyone was talking about how the king's son had been exchanged. Nevertheless, the people did not speak about it openly, lest the matter become known to the king. For after all, what could he possibly do about it? How could he undo what had been done? Besides, why should he believe such a tale? It might well be false. So, although people continued whispering the story about, it was felt that the king should not be told.

One day someone revealed the secret to the king's false son, telling him what people were saying about his having been exchanged. "Still," this person added, "I think it's beneath your dignity to investigate the matter. I'm only telling you this in case there's ever a conspiracy against the kingdom. The rumor could be advantageous to the conspirators. You ought to think about getting rid of this possible pretender."

The false prince began to harass the father of the other son, who was really his own father. He did the father injury whenever he could, for he wanted to cause him so much trouble that he would be compelled to take his son and depart. As long as the king was alive, the false prince had little power, but he still managed to make life difficult for his supposed rival. When the king grew old and died, the false prince succeeded him. He began to oppress the father of the other son more than ever, though he did this in such a way that no one would know what was going on, for such things would not seem right to the people.

The supposed father of the other son understood that he was being vexed because of the rumor about the exchange, and he told his supposed son the whole story. "I have great pity for you, whoever you are," he concluded. "If you are really my son, how can I help feeling sorry for you? And if you are not my son, but the son of the king, you are all the more to be pitied, for the false king will stop at nothing to get rid of you, God forbid. You must flee from this place."

This upset the youth greatly, but the new king continued to inflict so many hardships upon him that at last he decided to go into exile. His foster father gave him a considerable sum of money, and he departed.

The youth was very upset about being driven from his country for no reason. He considered his situation. "What have I done to deserve exile? If I am the king's son, I certainly should not be treated like this. And if I am not the king's son, I have done no evil, and there is no reason for me to be cast out." In his bitterness he took to drinking and frequenting brothels, desiring nothing more than to spend his time gratifying his desires.

Meanwhile the new king governed the land firmly. Whenever he heard of people who were gossiping about the rumored exchange of infants, he punished them severely and vengefully. He ruled by force and by might.

One day the false king went hunting with his court. They came upon a delightful spot by the river and paused there to rest. The king too lay down to rest, and thoughts of the other son whom he had unfairly driven out came into his mind. Whoever the other was, he had been wronged. If he was really a prince, was it not bad enough that he had been exchanged? Did he have to be exiled as well? And if he was not the king's son, there was also no reason for him to have been banished, for he had done no wrong. The king pondered and regretted his sin and the wicked thing he had done, but he could not make up his mind what to do about it. As there was nobody with whom he could discuss the matter, he became very uneasy. He told his officers that he wished to return home, for he had no more heart for sport. However, when he was back in the palace, he busied himself with his affairs, and the matter slipped from his mind.

The banished son continued to do as he pleased and squandered all his money. One day when he was walking by himself, he lay down to rest and recalled all that had befallen him. "What has God done to me?" he said to himself. "If I am a king's son, it is certainly not right for me to be an exile. And if I am not a king's son, I also do not deserve such a fate." He considered the matter further. "On the other hand, if God is really able to exchange a king's son and have him suffer such sorrows, does it make sense for me to behave as I do? Is it right to do as I have done?" He began to regret his evil ways, but after he returned home he went back to his life of dissipation.

Nevertheless, thoughts of regret and repentance continued to disturb him. One night he dreamed that a fair was going to be held in a certain place. He was to go there and accept the first task offered him, no matter how difficult and menial it seemed to be.

The dream made a strong impression on him. Generally when one wakes such things slip away immediately, but this dream stuck in his mind. Even so, it seemed too difficult for him to carry out, and he returned to his drinking as before. But the dream recurred several times, and it weighed heavily upon him.

One night in the dream a voice said to him, "If you know what's good for you, you'll do as you're told." So he set out to obey the dream. He gave what was left of his money and his fine clothes to the inn, and, taking for himself the simple dress of a peddler, he left for the fair.

He arrived at the place, and next morning he rose early and

went to the fair itself. Quite soon a merchant tapped him on the shoulders, saying, "Do you want to hire yourself out?"

"Yes," he answered.

"I have to drive some cattle," the merchant went on. "Come and work for me."

Because of what he had been told in the dream, the youth did not pause to consider the matter; he agreed at once. The merchant immediately started ordering him around in the manner of a master to his servant, and the youth soon had second thoughts. He was a gentle person and not suited for such work, and now he would have to drive cattle and tramp on foot alongside the beasts. But it was too late for him to change his mind, and the merchant continued ordering him about.

He asked his new master, "How can I go alone with the animals?"

The merchant answered, "There are other drovers looking after my cattle. You will go with them."

He gave him some cattle, and the youth drove them out of the city to the place where the other drovers were gathered. From there they all moved off together, with the youth among them, driving the animals that had been assigned to him. The merchant rode among the drovers on horseback and treated them roughly, and he was especially cruel to the youth. The youth was terrified of the merchant and feared that he would die on the spot if the merchant struck him even one blow with his stick. He was so soft and gentle that he felt he could not bear it.

In this way they continued, he with his animals and the merchant riding among the drovers. They came to a particular place and picked up a sack of bread that had been left for the drovers, and the merchant distributed the food among them. The youth was also given some of this bread, and he ate it.

Then they came to a very thick forest. Shortly after they had entered it, two of the animals that the youth was driving strayed away. The merchant shouted at him, and he ran after them to try to catch them. They fled even more, and he pursued them. Soon the cattle drovers could not see one another because the forest was so thick, and the youth was quickly separated from his companions. The farther he chased the animals, the more they ran away. He chased them on and on, until he came to the very depths of the forest, and there he paused to consider his situation: "One way or another, I shall die. If I return without the animals, the merchant will kill me, and if I remain here, I shall be eaten by wild beasts. Perhaps even so I should go back to the merchant. But how can I, without the animals?" He was so afraid of the merchant that he took up his chase once more, and the animals continued to flee.

Night fell. He had never before experienced anything like being alone in the night in the depths of the forest. When he heard the wild beasts howling, as they usually do, he decided to climb a tree. He slept there with the wild beasts' cries sounding in his ears.

In the morning he looked around and saw his cattle standing nearby. He climbed down in order to catch them, but the moment he approached them they ran away. He pursued them, but again they took flight. On and on he chased the animals, and on and on they fled. At times the animals would find some grass and stop to eat. Then he would draw near them and try to catch them, but they always managed to elude him. He followed them into the deepest part of the forest, where there lived wild animals that had no fear of man, so far away were they from human habitation.

Night fell again, and when he heard the wild beasts howling all around him, he became very frightened. He saw a very large tree standing nearby and began climbing it. When he came up into the tree, he saw a man lying there among the branches. He was frightened, but even so it relieved him to meet another human being.

"Who are you?" he asked.

"A man," replied the stranger. "And who are you?"

"A man."

"Where are you from?" asked the stranger.

The youth did not want to tell him the whole story, and so he said only: "I was a drover, and two animals that strayed from the herd led me here. But tell me, how did you come to be here?"

"My horse brought me here," the man replied. "I went out riding, and when I dismounted in order to rest, the horse wandered off into the forest. I chased him, but he kept running away from me, and that's how I come to be here."

The two decided to join forces and to remain together always, even when they returned to human habitation.

At dawn they heard a very powerful laugh resounding among the trees. It reverberated throughout the entire forest. It was so loud that even the tree in which they were sitting shook and trembled.

The youth was very frightened, but the man whom he had met in the tree said: "I am no longer afraid of this sound, because I have already spent several nights here. Every night toward dawn, as the darkness draws back, this laughter is heard, and all the trees shake and tremble."

The youth became very alarmed, and said to his companion, "This place must be inhabited by spirits, for such laughter is never heard in any place where humans live. Whoever heard of a laugh resounding over the whole world?"

Then suddenly it was day. They looked around and saw the animals of the youth and also the horse of his companion standing nearby. They climbed down the tree and began their pursuit, the youth after his animals and the other after his horse. The animals again fled before the youth as he ran after them, and the horse similarly eluded his master. Meanwhile the two wandered far apart from each other.

In the course of the chase, the youth found a sack filled with bread. Now bread is very important in the wilderness, so he took the sack and slung it up on his shoulder before continuing to follow the animals. On his way he met a man. He was very frightened at first, but even so he was somewhat relieved to meet another human being.

The man asked him, "How did you get here?"

The youth returned his question, "How did *you* get here?"

The man replied, "I, my fathers, and my forefathers were brought up in this place. But you, how did you ever find your way here? No one from where humans live ever comes here."

The youth was very frightened, because he realized that this man was not a human being at all. He had said that his forefathers were brought up here, and no one from where humans live ever came here. But the man of the forest did him no harm and was even rather friendly.

He asked the youth, "What are you doing here?"

The youth answered that he was chasing some stray animals.

"Stop chasing your sins," said the man. "It is not cattle but your sins that are leading you on. You have already been punished enough, so stop your pursuit. Come with me, and you will come into your own."

The king's true son accompanied him, but he was afraid to talk or ask anything, lest the man open his mouth and devour him. So he followed in silence, and on the way he met his comrade who had gone in pursuit of the horse. He warned him with signs: "This is not a human being. Have nothing to do with him."

Meanwhile his comrade had noticed the sack of bread on his shoulders, and entreated, "My brother, I have not eaten for several days. Give me some bread."

The youth replied, "Here in the wilderness my own life comes first, and I need the bread for myself."

The other continued begging and pleading, "I will give you anything you want for it."

The youth answered, "What can you give me in return for bread in the wilderness?"

"I will give you my entire self," replied the owner of the horse. "I'll sell myself to you as a bondservant."

The youth decided that it was a good bargain, and so he bought the other to be his bondservant for all time. His comrade swore that, in exchange for some bread, he would continue to serve him even when they returned to civilization. The only condition was that they would both eat from the sack until it was empty. So the two went on together, both following the man of the forest, with the horseman, who was now a servant, following the true son of the king. Having a servant made the journey a little easier for the youth. Whenever he needed to lift or do something, he would command his servant to lift it or to do whatever it was he wanted.

They came to a place that was crawling with snakes and scorpions. The youth was very frightened, so much so that he dared to speak to the man of the forest. "How will we ever get past this place?" he asked him.

"Why don't you also ask how you will be able to enter my house?" the man replied, and he showed them his house, which was suspended in midair.

They went on with him, and he brought them safely to his house. He gave them food and drink, and then he went away.

The king's true son used his servant whenever he needed anything. The servant was very bitter about having sold himself because of a single hour when he had needed bread. Now he had plenty to eat, but he would be a servant forever. He heaved a great sigh: "What have I come to? That I should be a servant!"

"Why are you moaning so much about being a servant?" asked the youth. "What kind of great position did you have before?"

The servant answered that he had once been a king. There had been a rumor about his having been exchanged and so forth, as was related before (for this was none other than the son of the serving maid), and he had driven out the other son. After a while it had occurred to him that he had been unjust, and he regretted it. He kept feeling sorry about the wicked deed that he had committed against the other son. One day he dreamed that the way to right the wrong was to relinquish his kingdom and travel as chance would take him, and in this way he would be able to make amends. He had not wanted to do this, but the dream recurred time and time again and upset him so much that he decided to obey. He abdicated his throne and wandered about until he finally ended up here—and now he had become a servant.

The other youth listened to the whole story in silence, thinking to himself, "I'll know how to deal with you."

In the evening the man of the forest returned and gave them food and drink, and they spent the night there.

Just before the day dawned, they heard the tremendous laugh that made the whole forest tremble. The servant urged the king's son to ask the man of the forest what was going on. So the youth asked him, "What is the great laugh that is heard at dawn?"

"That is the sound of the day laughing at the night," answered the man of the forest. "The night asks the day, 'Why is it that whenever you come, I no longer have a name?' The day bursts out laughing, and the night becomes day. That is the laughter that you hear at dawn. . . ."

This seemed a great marvel to the king's son, that the day should laugh at the night. But he could not ask any more questions, because of the man's amazing answer.

With morning the man of the forest departed again, and during the day the two companions ate and drank together in the house. When night fell the man returned, and they ate and drank and spent the night there. At night they heard the sound of the wild beasts roaring and making strange noises. The lion roared, the leopard howled, and the birds whistled and screeched, each and every beast making its own sound.

At first the two were frightened, and they did not listen to the sound attentively. Eventually they did begin to listen carefully, and they found that they were listening to a melody. The animals were singing a wonderful song. So marvelously pleasant was this music that the more they listened to it the more agreeable did it seem, till they felt that all the pleasures in the world could not compare with the pleasure of listening to it. They told each other that they should remain where they were in the forest, for there they had food and drink and this wonderful sweet music that surpassed all the pleasures in the world.

The servant urged his master to ask the man of the forest about the music. The youth asked him, and he replied, "The sun makes a garment for the moon. The creatures of the forest are very grateful to the moon, since the dominion of the beasts is mainly the night. Sometimes they have to enter the dwelling places of men, and they cannot do this by day. Because the moon does them the great favor of lighting up the night for them, they decided to compose a new song for the moon. This is the music that you hear."

Now that they knew it was a song, they listened to the music even more intently than before and were more impressed than ever with its wonderful sweetness. But the man of the forest said to them, "Why do you find this unique? I have an instrument made of leaves and colored things that I inherited from my forefathers, who inherited it from their ancestors. Whenever this instrument is placed on any bird or beast, it immediately begins to play this same wonderful melody."

After this, the great laughter was heard again, and it became day. The man of the forest left, and the true son of the king began to look for the instrument. He searched all over the room, but he did not find it. He did not dare go any farther.

The two were afraid to ask the man of the forest to lead them to a place where men lived. However, the man himself said that he would direct them to human habitation. Then he took out the instrument of which he had spoken and gave it to the king's true son.

"I give you this instrument as a gift," he said. "Now you must know how to master it."

The two then asked him, "Which way should we go?"

He answered that they must seek out the country called "the foolish country with the wise king." They asked him in which direction they should set out to begin asking for this country. He showed them the way with his hand, and then he told the real son of the king, "Go to that country, and there you will come into your greatness."

They set out. On their way they looked out for some creature on which they could try out the instrument to see if it would play, but they encountered no living being. Later, as they neared a town, they found an animal. They placed the instrument on it, and it began to play the music. They went on and on in this way, until they came to the country they were looking for.

The country was surrounded by a wall and could be entered only by way of one gate. In order to get to this gate one had to go around the wall for several miles. They went around until they reached the gate, but when they got there they were not permitted to enter. The king of the country had died. Although he had a son to succeed him, the king had left a will in which he had written that whereas the kingdom had previously been called "the foolish country with the wise king," now it should be called the reverse, "the wise country with the foolish king." Whoever restored the former name to the kingdom, so that it would be again called "the foolish country with the wise king" —he would become king. So no one was permitted to enter the country unless he first undertook to restore the former name to the kingdom. "Can you undertake this task?" they asked the youth. He could not, and so the two could not enter. The servant urged his master to turn back, but he did not wish to, because the man of the forest had told him to go to this country in order to come into his greatness.

Meanwhile another man arrived, riding on a horse. He also wanted to enter, but they would not let him in for the same reason. Seeing the man's horse, the king's son took out his instrument. He placed it on the horse, and it immediately began to play the very marvelous melody. The man on the horse begged him to sell him the instrument, but the youth did not want to part with it.

"What can you possibly give me in return for this marvelous instrument?" he asked.

The man on the horse replied, "What can you do with this instrument of yours? Perhaps you can make a show with it, and someone will throw you a gold coin. But I know something better than your instrument, something that I received from my forefathers, with which one is able to comprehend one thing from another. If someone says a single word, it is possible, by means of this secret knowledge that has been handed down to me, to comprehend one thing from another. I have not yet revealed this knowledge to anyone in the world, but I am willing to teach it to you if you will give me that instrument."

The king's true son decided that it would indeed be a wonderful thing to be able to comprehend one thing from another, and he gave him the instrument. The man on the horse then taught him how to comprehend one thing from another.

The king's true son then returned to the gate in the wall, for he realized that he could now undertake to restore to the country its former name. He did not know how he was going to do this, but as he now was able to comprehend one thing from another, he realized that it could be done. Besides, what could he lose by trying? When he told the people at the gate that he would undertake the task, they allowed him to enter.

The chief ministers were informed that someone had come who would undertake the task, and the youth was brought before them. They told him, "Know that we also are not fools, God forbid! It's just that the former king was a very great sage, and in comparison with him we were all fools. That is why the land used to be called 'the foolish country with the wise king.' With the passing of the king, his son, who is also a sage, has taken over the throne. In comparison with us, however, he is not at all wise, and therefore the kingdom is now called 'the wise country with the foolish king.' In his will the old king stated that when we find a man so wise that he can restore to the country its former name, we should make him king. Such a man must be so wise that by comparison all of us are fools. When he becomes king, the country can again be called 'the foolish country with the wise king.' The former king made it plain that his son was to relinquish the throne and turn over the kingdom to such a man when he appeared. Know then what you are undertaking."

The ministers went on, "The test of whether you are such a sage is this: there is a garden that was left by the former king. It is a very wondrous garden, in which grow vessels made of metal—of silver and of gold. But it is impossible to enter this garden, for whenever someone enters it, he is immediately pursued. He is pursued and he cries out—but he doesn't know or see who is pursuing him. In this way he is pursued until he is driven from the garden. This is how we shall see how wise you are: we shall see whether you can enter the garden."

The young man asked whether the person who entered was beaten.

The ministers answered, "The main thing is that he is pursued and doesn't know by whom, and he flees in great terror. So we have been told by those who have entered the garden."

The youth went out toward the garden. He saw that there was a wall around it, but the gate was open and there were no guards. To be sure, there was no need to watch over this garden! As he approached, he looked about him and saw a man, or rather the statue of a man, standing near the garden. He looked again and noticed an inscribed tablet stating that this man had been king hundreds of years ago, and that in his days there had been peace, but before his time and after it there had been war. Since the son had learned to comprehend one thing from another, he realized that everything depended upon this man, and that if he entered the garden and was pursued, there was no need to flee. All he had to do was to stand near this man and he would be safe. Moreover, if this man was moved and placed inside the garden, it would be possible for anyone to enter safely. The king's son entered the garden, and as soon as he felt that he was being pursued, he went over and stood next to the man just outside the gate. In this way he came out in peace and unharmed. Others who had entered the garden had become terrified and fled as soon as the pursuit began, and so they had been vanquished. The king's son, by standing next to the man, came out in peace and unharmed.

The ministers saw this and were astonished. The young man then gave instructions to have the statue moved into the garden. When this had been done, all of the ministers entered the garden and came out of it in peace.

Then the ministers told the son, "Although we have seen what you have accomplished, you cannot yet be given the kingdom. We shall give you one more test. The throne of the former king is very high. Various birds and beasts all carved of wood stand around it. In front of the throne there is a bed, next to the bed there is a table, and on the table is a lamp. Many roads, all paved in stone, extend in all directions from where the throne stands. No one knows the meaning of this throne and the roads. At a certain distance out along one of the roads there is a golden lion which opens its mouth and devours anyone who approaches. The road continues beyond the lion. It is the same with all the other roads, each of which leads in a different direction. On the second road there is a leopard—also made of metal. And so it is with all the other roads, which extend throughout the entire country, each with its metal beast. No one understands the meaning of the throne or the objects on the road around it. You will be proven by whether you can comprehend all these things."

Then they showed him the throne, and he saw that it was indeed very high. He approached it and examined it more closely, and he noticed that it was made of the same material as was the instrument that the man of the forest had given him.

He looked again and noticed that on the topmost part of the throne a rose was missing. He understood that if this rose were in its place the throne would have the same power as the instrument which played music whenever it was placed on an animal or a bird. He looked even more closely and saw that the missing rose was in fact lying beneath the throne. Were it picked up and set back on high, the throne would have the power of the marvelous instrument. The former king had arranged and hidden everything with such subtlety that no man could understand it, until such time as a very wise man came. He would understand it all and be able to put everything back in its place.

In the same way, the king's son realized that the bed had to be shifted a little from where it was standing. The table also had to be moved a little, and also the lamp. In addition, each of the birds and the beasts had to be put in its proper place. One must take this bird and put it in that place, and so with all the other beasts. The king had arranged everything with cunning and wisdom, in such a way that no one would be able to comprehend it all until that wise man came who would restore things to their proper order. The lion at the turning of the road also had to be set elsewhere, and so with all the other beasts on all the other roads.

The young man commanded that everything be put back in the proper order: the rose was to be picked up from beneath the throne and set back on high, and all the other things were to be moved around and arranged in their proper order according to his directions. When all was done as he had instructed, everything began to give forth the sweetest and most marvelous music. Each object did what it was supposed to do. Then they gave him the kingdom.

And the true son who had now become king said to the son of the maid, "Now I understand that I am indeed the true son of the king, and you are the true son of the maid."

Commentary

Like many of Rabbi Nachman's stories, "The King's Son and the Son of the Maid" can be read in a number of ways. It is an allegory rich in kabbalistic symbolism. A number of different sets of keys to the symbolism have been proposed. In the following interpretation the story is seen as a description of man's spiritual struggle with himself, a struggle that takes place entirely within the confines of the human soul. Another, totally different explanation, not elaborated upon here, is that the tale is a depiction of the fate of the Jewish people, a new rendering of the ancient tale between Jacob and Esau.

According to the Kabbalah (in the form expressed in hasidic literature), each man possesses two souls, one animal, the other divine. The animal spirit is the vital force that gives life to the body, though it possesses in addition spiritual components that are oriented beyond this function and do not exist purely as ends in themselves. The divine soul reflects the pure inner essence of humanity, its yearning toward the divine; it is unconnected to the body or its needs, which, indeed, it frequently overcomes. It aspires to be and do good.

Every man's life is an ongoing struggle between these two souls, each of which strives to capture and dominate the individual. The tale of the "king's son"—the divine soul—and the "maid's son"—the animal soul—describes such a struggle. The ups and downs of the human spirit are traversed, from the inner torment of self-knowledge and the struggle for a correct relationship between the two souls, through sufferings of regret and repentance. Divine and animal are drawn into the mysterious forest of the soul's confusion, and a way out of this confusion is found. The concluding section describes the divine soul's way toward a higher solution of the world's problems.

The basic plot of this story is essentially original, although some of the subsidiary themes, which are linked together in a string of episodes, are familiar to us from folktales. The symbolism and allegory were strongly influenced (as Rabbi Nachman himself points out in an appendix to the story, not printed here) by the Kabbalah, especially its most ancient tradition of "chariot" mysticism.

THE KINGS AND THE SONS

From the time of the Bible, Jewish literature has used the image of the king to represent God. Rabbi Nachman's stories use this imagery too, though, typically, divine intervention is not a feature of the plot.

The child born to the queen is the king's true offspring and represents the divine soul. This is in keeping with the concept that the divine soul is "part of God." The relation of the other son to the king is problematic. It is inconceivable that a created being should not be related in some way with the Divine, and the animal soul is presented as a member of the royal household —the son of one of the king's servants. The two sons are born at the same time, for when the body is born, both souls, like twins, enter the world and begin the saga of life together.

THE EXCHANGE

The two children are dependent on each other, and the one cannot exist without the other. The divine soul needs the animal soul in order to live, and the animal soul needs the divine soul in order to find direction. However, normal relations depend on the king's son being the ruler—a natural state which is disturbed by the unfortunate exchange.

The exchange seems to be almost capricious, but it is the "mistake" that occurs at every man's birth: the animal soul is placed in an advantageous position relative to the divine soul. Furthermore, everyone, including the individual himself, is convinced that the animal soul is in fact the king's son who governs the kingdom by right. The divine soul is thrust into a subordinate position and kept there by the pressure of public opinion.

The two souls grow up and study together, but they learn different things. The maid's son who grows up as a king's son has to learn to restrain himself in order to rule; in other words, the social and human condition refines the animal soul. Nevertheless, he tends to return to his own nature, for although there are many advantages to sitting on a throne, there is also a fascination in being a servant.

It is important to note that the maid's son is not described in disparaging terms; the animal part of man is neither "evil" nor "dark." In fact he possesses some positive traits, and he is clearly successful and adept in practical matters, certainly no less than the other son. The king's true son is also uncomfortable in his role and aspires to the kingship even in his subservient position.

The source of the problem is the exchange. Its development and resolution can begin only when the secret is revealed and reaches consciousness. Disclosure is inevitable, because the noble-divine part of the soul cannot live indefinitely in a subordinate position. The whispering of the people is the first stage of disclosure. This is the vague feeling of discontent, the first, faint awareness of a higher destiny for the true son and of an honest, subordinate fate for the maid's son.

The second stage begins when the matter reaches the consciousness of the animal soul. Talebearers are associated with the "evil inclination," for they awaken the evil that can develop from the animal soul and place it in opposition to good; nevertheless, what the talebearer says is the truth. Once the secret is out, the two sons no longer live together in peace. The spurious prince is warned that the matter should not be investigated, for any such inquiry could reveal his unfitness for the throne. Fear of exposure leads to the stifling of real thought. Characteristic of this situation is the fact that the two sons can continue to live together only as long as they have no awareness of their true identity and of the differences between them. This is a feature of childhood: the distinction between good and evil is still obscure.

The antagonism between the material and the spiritual is perceived first by the animal soul, and, oddly enough, only later by the nobler side. The false son takes the initiative, and, in his effort to get rid of the king's real son, launches an attack against the servant who is, in fact, his own father. This character represents common sense, which is the real father of man's animal nature, engendering those aspects of its soul that enable it to rule over the whole soul.

THE DEATH OF THE KING
AND THE EXILE OF THE TRUE SON

While the king is still alive, the maid's son cannot gain complete control. When he dies—in other words, when man says that there is no God and that he alone rules the universe— the false king can ascend to the throne. The false king now feels free to act, though he is still restrained to a certain extent by public opinion. He cannot yet cast off the burden of spirituality altogether, but he continues and intensifies the oppression in secret. The weight of the personality as a whole leans increasingly toward the physical world. Eventually, the very presence of the divine soul becomes intolerable, and the true son is exiled.

The king's son is banished, but man's spirituality cannot disappear altogether, and it is now manifest in a terrible bitterness that leads the individual to drunkenness, riotous living, and the brothel. In themselves the natural appetites are not extreme. It is not lust that drives a man to excess; drunkenness and dissipation are symptoms of a condition in which the soul yearns for something pure and exalted but cannot cope with the realities of the human existence.

THE TWO SONS BEGIN TO REPENT

At first the animal soul is not affected by the banishment of the divine soul. The false king rules successfully and material welfare is attained. Any intimation that all is not well is either held in contempt or fiercely suppressed. The false king rules with a firm hand.

This is the stage of ambivalence. Neither of the sons is a clear-cut "good" or "evil" character. One aspires for the noble and the divine and yet acts in the opposite direction, while the other is not unwavering or even at ease with his worldliness.

The animal soul does endeavor—as perhaps every man does during the storm and fury of adolescence—to build a harmonious life out of the jagged principles of materialism. In a moment of leisure, however, he comes to the realization that something is lacking in his existence as a human being, and he misses his counterpart. Ultimately matter seeks only comfort and does not aspire to kingship; in the depths of its being it wishes to be led firmly toward the sublime. Thus, at moments of respite from his royal duties, the false king does begin to repent. In order to get rid of this uncomfortable emotion, he returns to his routine, finding forgetfulness in activity.

Paralleling the false king's spiritual crisis, there is an awakening in the true son, an awareness of his royal heritage and of a deep need to realize himself. The point of departure is the very bitterness that had driven him to dissipation. The clear wish for a nobler cause is still unformed, but the first step is made toward it. Thus, bitterness can be a constructive factor: sin can be overcome, and one can return to confront the basic aims of life.

THE TRUE SON'S SECOND EXILE

A single disagreeable encounter with the truth is not enough to initiate the process of repentance, and it is repeated through the medium of a dream. The true son is told that he is to abandon his sinful way of life, that he must change completely. When this dream recurs, a crisis develops, and eventually he obeys and sets out to face his uncertain destiny.

When he leaves on his second exile, the true son has already freed himself from an impossible situation, though his new status of cattledrover to a cruel master is also unenviable. There is, however, a great difference between the two conditions: previously chasing animals (or animality) had given him pleasure, whereas now it is a source of misery. The cruel merchant is a symbol of evil in many of Rabbi Nachman's stories. The dual role of evil—both tempter and punisher—is found in talmudic sources. The cruel merchant forces the son to cling to his previous mode of life. This reflects the Jewish conception of punishment, which is seen as the endless repetition of one's sins when they have lost their attraction and every further pleasure is accompanied by increasing misery.

When two of the beasts run away, the tension reaches a climax. The true son cannot overcome the illusion that he has to follow them. He cannot live with them, and he cannot live without them. Man is in mortal fear of his master, his habits.

THE FOREST, A PARTIAL SOLUTION

The forest is a whole world of mystery, the innermost recess of the human soul; here man experiences the enigmatic, the inexplicable, and perceives mysterious images of himself and the world. Rabbi Nachman uses a well-known kabbalistic symbol of the forest as "the world of the angels"—a higher realm of existence. Here the two sons, having arrived by different but parallel paths, meet again and start to build a new relationship. The image of "the man on the horse" is an enlargement of the biblical verse: "I have seen servants upon horses, And princes walking as servants upon the earth" (Eccles. 10: 7).

The first step in the establishment of this new relationship (in the establishment of proper order in the soul) is the acquisition of the sack of bread. The bread is a symbol of divine wisdom, and possessing it gives the true son a unique advantage. Next is the meeting between the true son and the spirit of the forest, who helps the true son to find himself. He begins by releasing him from the pursuit of the animals and revealing its significance. The fact that the spirit of the forest is not human shows that he is of the class of the angelic beings, to which the king's true son is by nature closely related. In the symbolism of the Kabbalah, the "spirit of the forest" is an angel who is, in fact, the "master" of this particular world.

In the forest of the soul, man can encounter other aspects of himself, and it is here that the true son meets the man who is pursuing his horse (a pursuit which is symbolic of the sin and the punishment of the usurper king). The false son is incapable of establishing direct contact with the spirit of the forest; his blindness to mystical revelation is evident. He is entirely dependent on the true son, who possesses the bread, and, as a result, is forced to become his bondservant forever. Once the correct relationship between the two souls is established, it cannot be altered.

The spirit takes them through the forest, through the inner complexities of the soul, into terrible, incomprehensible places, past great spiritual dangers, the "snakes and scorpions." They doubt if they will ever emerge. However, there is a way through, and when the king's son submits to the spirit of the forest, perhaps an aspect of his own inner forces, he finds himself again in a "house" which, though it is suspended in midair, is a recognizable feature, a small, rational world in the depth of the forest.

The servant encourages his master to ask questions. There is no evil intention in this. As part of the new, healthy relationship that has been established, the servant offers his skills and talents for the benefit of the other. The divine soul tends, by nature, to be quietistic and passive, while the animal soul has the powers of curiosity and inquiry which lead to action and achievement.

The first question concerns the tremendous laugh that is heard before dawn. The spirit of the forest explains that the laugh is the joyous sound of good. The light of day is divine revelation, the positive, genuine aspect of reality. Night, darkness, is the evil that holds back the manifestation of revelation. So long as the night endures, it appears to be no less real than the day, but in fact evil is only negative existence, the absence of good. It has no name. When light does eventually come—and come it must, even if, like Redemption, it tarries—it thrusts out darkness completely. Night evaporates without a struggle, and those who had clung to it wonder what happened to its apparent fullness of existence. Then day speaks in a great burst of laughter, the triumphant, joyful laughter of good.

Other strange sounds are heard in the forest, such as the cries of the beasts. This is the sound of primordial nature, which at first terrifies all who hear it. Gradually, however, one can learn to distinguish separate sounds within the mighty roar and, eventually, perhaps, to perceive the profound, overwhelmingly beautiful harmony. One may also reach an ecstatic enjoyment, the bliss of being in touch with the very essence of life. This is the greatest pleasure in the world.

Nevertheless man desires not only to experience phenomena, but also to understand them, and the spirit of the forest is questioned about the harmony. The second answer also touches upon the very root of things. "The sun makes a garment for the moon." In the symbolism of the Kabbalah, the sun represents the divine plenty, while the moon is the *Shekhinah*, the divine power that distributes the abundance of life to the world. The moon has no light of its own, and it merely reflects what it receives from the sun. The creatures are incapable of absorbing the sun's light, which is so bright that it blots out worldly reality, and they must receive their life-illumination indirectly from the moon. They are thus indebted to the moon and render it homage and love. So when the sun "makes a garment for the moon," that is, when divine revelation is passed on to the world, all life voices a universal song of praise and thanksgiving to its apparent source. The blissful response to this sound derives from a mystical vision of unity, an awareness of oneness.

The instrument possessed by the spirit of the forest is a kind of mystical knowledge. By putting together leaves and colored fragments, symbolic of the separate parts of the forest, its owner can contain the great harmony and extract it from every living creature. He can reveal the totality of nature that is contained in every detail. However, this music, despite its beauty and its magic, ultimately belongs to the world of night that conceals the divine spirit. Man cannot dwell indefinitely in this world of private mysticism and must emerge, after the rehabilitation of his soul, into social reality.

The King's Son and the Son of the Maid

FROM THE FOREST OF THE SOUL
TO THE WORLD OF MEN

The spirit of the forest prepares the divine soul, now the master, for this next stage of the journey. He warns him that he must exert firm control, neither too severe nor too lax, over his servant and gives him three gifts: the instrument, representing the essence of his sojourn in the forest, a destination, and instructions on how to reach it.

Emergence from the forest is separation from one realm of existence and entry into another. It is a kind of rebirth, the return to the world of a better-balanced and integrated personality. The true son is now ready to undertake his great task, to seek out "the wise country with the foolish king" and reinstate its old name, "the foolish country with the wise king." He must reverse the decline which had set in when the old king died, and must restore to the country its previous glory. The message is clear: after the state of the soul has been put right, one must correct the world.

A CHOICE: BEAUTY OR TRUTH

The meeting with the man on horseback is of profound importance, and it represents a telling attack on being satisfied with the enjoyment of beauty and of mystical experience and on regarding the blissful feeling of harmony as an end in itself. This state is indeed a source of unparalleled pleasure for the fortunate who can attain it, but ultimately it is valueless and adds nothing to the stature of man. The man on the horse asks: "What can you do with this instrument of yours? Perhaps you can make a show with it, and someone will throw you a gold coin." In its place he offers the wisdom he received from his fathers—the ability to comprehend one thing from another. This is the Torah, in its broadest sense, which includes the knowledge and the wisdom of the Kabbalah. The Torah is much more than a textbook of legal and moral precepts: it is a God-given means of understanding the inner significance of the world. Whereas the instrument expresses the harmony of untamed nature, the Torah seeks to change nature and improve it, even struggle against it. The king's son makes his choice and is ready to approach the task, which is explained by the elders of the city.

THE WISE COUNTRY
WITH THE FOOLISH KING

In the beginning the king (God) established the kingdom (the created world). As long as he himself governed, the country was known as "the foolish country with the wise king," for no matter how well the ministers managed the country, they could never approach his wisdom. However, after the Creation, God appears to withdraw from the world and wills it to His son, man, who is inadequate and admits that he is "a foolish king over a wise country." The country, however, desires to return to its original status and seeks a human ruler who will be able to perform this task of restoration. Ultimately, this task is incumbent on every human being. The king left certain inherent flaws in the kingdom, so that men would be able to correct them and restore the world to perfection.

The first test for the prospective redeemer is to unravel the mystery of the "garden," which symbolizes *Pardes*, Jewish esoteric wisdom. It is also the Garden of Eden, which cannot be penetrated by ordinary men, even though it is open and all can approach it and attempt to enter. The true son notices the open gate and seeks to understand the perils of the garden.

The solution he finds is the statue of a man by the gate. This figure may be identified by the inscription that "in his days there had been peace, but before his time and after it there had been war." This clearly refers to King Solomon, who possessed divine wisdom. *Pardes* is a dangerous place, and no man may find his way in it so long as he tries to grasp things as they appear to be. The greatest difficulty in comprehending esoteric wisdom is that its symbols are viewed as realities and the allegory is not perceived. By standing next to the figure of Solomon, the true son acquires Solomon's profound perception and insight into the esoteric symbols. When the statue is placed within the garden—that is, when the world is comprehended by esoteric allegory—he and all men may enter and leave the garden safely.

Having achieved this understanding, the true son can set about the second, even greater task of setting the world right, using his new knowledge, in a series of symbolic acts. The esoteric aspect of the world is known in Jewish mysticism as the "chariot," and, indeed, the whole world is regarded, in a way, as God's throne or chariot. The throne in the story is the seat of the former king, which is described in terms reminiscent of mystical passages in the Bible. It is very high ["I saw the Lord sitting upon a throne high and lifted up" (Isa. 6:1)] and surrounded by a number of creatures (Ezek. 1:5). Roads lead out from the throne—mysterious channels through which the divine abundance flows to the various worlds and their denizens. However, something is wrong with the throne, something is missing; furthermore, the lion, like other creatures in the world, has become a ferocious beast of prey, for it no longer receives radiance from the throne. The roads are blocked, and evil is present in the disordered world. Whosoever holds the esoteric key and can remedy the situation—he is the redeemer.

When he sets about reinstating order, the true son discovers that the throne is made of the same material as the wondrous instrument and understands that it too contains in itself the inner essence of the whole world. In the forest, the instrument represented the Ark of the Law, but there it contained no specific message. Here it corresponds to the Ark, but contains the Torah, which was regarded by Jewish sages of all ages as equivalent to the divine throne within the temple. The true son notices that certain details are out of place, each of them of kabbalistic significance. Thus the rose—which in the Zohar is interpreted as *Knesset Israel,* the quintessential community of Israel, and also the *Shekhinah,* God's presence in the world— has fallen and must be raised. It is interesting to note that nothing has to be moved very far. Shifting things just a little into their correct places is all that is required to reintroduce harmony.

The Torah provides guidance on correcting or mending the divine throne and makes it clear that only small adjustments are required, not destroying and remaking. These small symbolic adjustments, the minor changes in reality, are the *mitzvot.* Each individual *mitzvah* is only a minute part of the whole process, but when all the *mitzvot* are performed properly and at the right time, the whole world can be perfected. Many generations of the true sons of the king, busying themselves with these acts of correction, will bring about the redemption of the world.

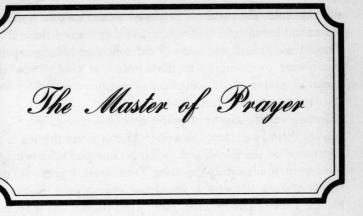

The Master of Prayer

ONCE there was a master of prayer who spent all his days in prayer, in singing hymns, and in praise of God. He lived in a secluded spot, far from the habitations of man.

From time to time he would visit a town, and he would enter the home of one of the humble and the poor. There he would talk about the true purpose of life, which, he would say, is to spend all one's days in the worship of God, in singing hymns, and in praises. He would speak thus until at last people desired to join him.

Such men the master of prayer would bring back with him to his secluded spot. A river flowed there, and there were trees of which they ate the fruits. As for their clothes, they did not mind what they wore. They spent their days in prayer and singing hymns and praises to God, and in confessions, fasting, and penitence. The master of prayer gave them his own books on prayer and hymns and confessions, and they studied these at all times. Time passed, and some of the followers became capable of drawing men's hearts to the worship of God. These the master of prayer would sometimes permit to go into the towns to arouse men to the worship of God.

In this way the master of prayer enticed people to serve God and led them away from the world. After a while this made an impression on the world, and then it became public knowledge. Men were suddenly disappearing from their homes. In one family it was a son who vanished and in another a son-in-law. No one knew where they had gone. Time passed, and it became known that there was a master of prayer who was going from place to place enticing people to leave the towns and join him in the worship of God. People wanted to catch him but could not, for he always appeared in a different guise: at one time as a beggar, at another as a merchant, and so on and so forth. Furthermore, when he perceived that the man he was talking to did not grasp his intention, he would so confuse the listener with words that he had no idea what the master of prayer desired. The master of prayer acted so cleverly that no one could catch him.

The master of prayer understood men's hearts and could provide each of his followers with what he needed. If he saw that one of them needed to wear garments embroidered with gold, he would provide them. But if it happened that a rich man joined him, and he needed to go around in tattered rags, he would provide these too. He knew what was necessary for each and every one. All the people whom the master of prayer had drawn to God found fasting and penance dearer to them than any worldly delight.

In those days there was a country of wealth. All its inhabitants were rich, but their customs were very strange. The measure of everything was money, and the importance and rank of every individual was determined by his wealth. A man who possessed so many thousands or millions was accorded a certain rank, and another who owned a different sum of money was of another rank, and so on and so forth. And he who possessed so and so many millions was king.

They also had flags. If someone possessed such-and-such a sum and was of such-and-such a rank, he was entitled to a special flag. Another, who possessed a different sum and was of a different rank, had another flag. It was clearly laid down how much money a person must possess in order to be of a particular rank and have a particular flag.

If a citizen of that country possessed no more than a certain sum of money, he was considered to be an ordinary human being. However, if he had less than that sum, he was held to be a beast or a bird in human form. There were various beasts and birds. One who possessed a certain small sum of money was a lion (that is, a human lion), and one who possessed even less was some kind of bird. In any event, a man with little money was not considered to be a human being.

It became known in the world that such a country existed. The master of prayer sighed and said, "Who knows how much farther this folly may lead them astray!" Some of his followers heard him and, without asking about it, decided to go to the country of wealth. They felt great pity for its people, who had strayed so far in their lust for money, especially since the master of prayer had said that those people might sink even deeper into error. So they went there in the hope that they would be able to turn the people back from their ways.

On reaching the country, they entered the home of one of the poorest people, a man who was considered to be a beast, and they began to converse with him. Wealth is not the highest value, they said, for the true purpose of life is to worship God. But the man took no heed of what they were saying, for the error was deeply rooted in his heart. So they went to another and repeated what they had said to the first. He too would not listen, and when they persisted, he said, "I have no time to talk with you."

"Why?" asked the followers.

"Because we are preparing to leave this country and go to another. Since we consider wealth to be the highest goal, we are moving to a country where money is made, where the soil contains ores of gold and silver."

The people of this country had also decided to appoint among themselves stars and constellations. Whosoever possessed such-and-such a sum of money was considered to have the power of a star. They believed that it was the influence of the stars that made gold grow in the earth, and so if a man was very rich, he must possess the same powers as did the stars; in other words, he was a star himself. Furthermore, if a man possessed even greater wealth than a star, he was regarded as an entire constellation of stars. They also appointed angels, all according to wealth, and finally they agreed that they should have gods, too. Whosoever possessed a certain immense sum of money, thousands of millions, must surely be a god. They said that if God had bestowed so much wealth upon him, he must surely be a god himself.

The people of the country of wealth also decided that it was not fitting that they should live in the air of this world. Nor should they mix with other inhabitants of the world, who were unclean, lest they become defiled by them. So they decided to seek out high mountains, the very highest in the world. There they would settle, and there they would live above the air of the world. So they sent out scouts, who discovered very high mountains, and they all went to live there. A different group settled on each peak. They built great fortifications and earthworks around each mountain so that no one could approach them. There was a single secret path leading up to each mountaintop, and no stranger could ever find it. They also placed watchmen at some distance from each mountain so that no stranger could approach them. And there they lived, observing their strange customs, and they had many gods, that is, gods according to wealth.

Since they valued money above all, they lived in perpetual fear of murder and robbery. After all, who would not become a criminal if by stealing money he could become a god? On the other hand, they thought that a god—that is, someone who possessed great wealth—would be able to protect himself.

They instituted rituals and sacrifices and prayers to these gods. They offered up human sacrifices, and people even sacrificed themselves in order to become one with the gods, hoping that thus they would be reborn as rich men.

Nevertheless, the country was plagued by murder and robbery, for whoever did not believe in the efficacy of the rites became a murderer and robber in order to get more money.

Money buys everything, they maintained: food, clothing, and the essentials of life are all acquired by means of money. That was why money was their religion. They made great efforts to ensure that they would never be without money, and they began to import wealth into their country. Merchants went out to trade in other lands and brought their profits home. Charity was, of course, a great sin, for who would be so wicked as to give away the money that God had bestowed upon him?

They also appointed officials whose task it was to ascertain whether each person had as much money as he declared. Everyone had to make regular statements of his wealth in order to retain his rank. When a rich person lost his money, he was demoted from the rank of man to that of animal, and when a poor man became rich, he was promoted from animal to man, and so with all the ranks.

They kept icons and portraits of their gods, that is, of men who possessed great wealth. Everyone kept such icons, which they fondled and kissed, for money was their sole object of worship and religion.

When the followers returned to their secluded spot, they told the master of prayer about the great folly of the country of wealth, how the people there had been led astray by their lust for money, and how some wanted to leave their own country for another where they would be able to make gold.

The master of prayer declared that he feared that the people of that country would fall into even greater folly. When he heard that they had appointed their own gods, he said, "That's just what I thought would happen! That's just what I feared!"

The master of prayer was very sorry for them, and he decided to go to that country, in the hope that he would be able to turn them from their folly. When he arrived, he spoke to the watchmen who were stationed around each of the mountains. These were obviously poor people of low status, for the rich who had attained higher rank refused to come into contact with ordinary humans, nor would they come down to the air of this world, for fear of pollution. They would not even talk with the people from the outside world, lest they be defiled by the breath of their mouths. So the watchmen who were stationed below the city were of low rank, but they too kept icons of their gods, for even they believed in the religion of money.

The master of prayer spoke to one of the watchmen about the true purpose of life, which, he explained, was the worship of God, through Torah, prayer, and good deeds. He said that money was pure folly. The watchman took no heed of what he said, so deeply rooted was his belief in money.

The master of prayer then approached the other watchmen and spoke to them in the same way, but none of them listened to him.

Then the master of prayer decided to go up to the city on the mountain. People were amazed to see him there. "How did you get in?" they asked him, for no outsider could enter.

"Why do you ask?" he answered. "It's enough that I'm here." Then he began to talk with one of them about the true purpose of life, declaring in his usual way that money was pure folly. This person took no heed of his words, and so it was with the next and the next. They had all sunk so deep into their folly that they would consider nothing else. The people of the city were astonished that there was a man among them saying things that were so completely opposed to their religion. They had heard of the master of prayer, for his activities were already well known, and they realized that this must be he. But they could not catch him, because he appeared to each in a different guise, and he quickly left the city.

In those days there was a warrior around whom had gathered a band of fighting men. They went around the world conquering countries. This warrior insisted that all the countries in the world submit themselves to him, but he sought nothing else. If a country did surrender, it suffered no injury; but if it resisted, it was destroyed. The warrior was not interested in money; he only wanted people to accept his rule. When he was at a distance of some fifty miles from the country, he would dispatch a group of his men to demand its surrender. In this way he conquered one country after another.

When the merchants of the country of wealth returned from their travels, they told the people about this warrior. The whole country was terrified. Although they wanted to surrender, they could not, for they had heard that the warrior despised money and wanted none of it. To surrender to such a man, who rejected their religion, would be apostasy.

In their great fear, the people started performing their religious rites, offering up animals (that is, men who had little money) as sacrifices to their gods (men who had much money). Meanwhile the warrior came nearer to the country, and, as was his custom, sent a group of his men to demand its surrender. The people were dreadfully frightened and did not know what to do. Then their merchants made a suggestion. In their travels they had heard about a country all of whose inhabitants "were gods who rode in carriages drawn by angels." That is, everyone there was so immensely wealthy that even the humblest of them would be considered a god in the country of wealth. Even their horses were bedecked with enough gold and other precious metals to make one an angel in the country of wealth, so, in effect, their carriages were drawn by angels. "They harness up three pairs of angels and ride off with them!" related the merchants. "They will be able to help us, for they are all gods." This advice pleased the people. They were certain that assistance would come from a country that was populated by gods.

The master of prayer decided to return to the country of wealth, in the hope that he might still be able to turn its people from their folly. When he arrived, he approached one of the watchmen and began to talk with him in his usual manner. The watchman told him about the warrior, of whom they were so terrified.

"What do you intend to do?" asked the master of prayer.

The watchman answered that they were going to send for help to the country that was inhabited by gods.

The master of prayer laughed heartily at his words. "That's utter nonsense!" he said. "They are merely men, like us. All of you, including your gods, are no more than men, and no man is a god. There is only one God over the world, He who created all. One must worship Him alone, and pray only to Him. This is the true and only purpose of life." The master of prayer continued talking in this way, but for a long time the watchman refused to listen, for the folly was deeply rooted in his heart. But the master of prayer persisted.

Eventually the watchman said, "But what can I do? I am one,

and they are many. . . ." This encouraged the master of prayer, for he realized that his earlier conversation with the same watchman and what he had just said were beginning to make an impression.

He went on to another watchman and spoke to him in the same way. This watchman, too, refused to listen, but finally he answered, "But I am one, and they are many. . . ." Eventually all the watchmen gave him the same answer.

Then the master of prayer went up to the city. He told the people that they were all in great error, and that money was not the aim of life, but that the true and only purpose of life was to occupy oneself with Torah and prayer. They, too, did not want to listen to him, so deeply rooted among them was the worship of money.

They told him of the warrior, and of how they intended to send for help to the country inhabited by gods. He laughed and told them that their plan was folly.

"They won't be able to help you at all," he told them, "for you are merely men, and they are merely men, not gods. There is only one God, blessed be He. . . ." But he said, as though talking to himself, "Can this be the warrior?" He went from one person to another, speaking to them all in the same way, and of the warrior he said to each, "Can this be the warrior?" No one knew what he meant by this.

Meanwhile, the presence in the city of a man who mocked their religion and said that there is only one God, and who said that perhaps he knew the warrior, was creating a great stir. People realized that he must surely be the famous master of prayer. An order was given to seek him out and seize him. He continued to use his different disguises, but they were already known, and finally he was caught.

The master of prayer was brought before the elders, and they began to talk with him. He spoke to them in the same way as he had to the others: "You are all in error, and you have strayed into great folly. Money is not the true purpose of life. There is only one God, blessed be His name, who has created all, and one must worship Him alone. Money is folly and nothing more. And as for that country which you say is inhabited by gods, you will get no help from them, for they are not gods, but men, as you are." They thought he was mad, for anyone who did not accept their folly seemed to them to be mad.

"Why do you keep saying, 'Can this be the warrior?' " they asked him.

"I was once in the service of a king," he answered, "and it happened that one day the king's warrior was lost. If this is the same warrior, I know him. Furthermore, putting your trust in the country you claim is inhabited by gods is folly. They will not be able to help you. On the contrary, putting your trust in them will bring about your downfall."

"How do you know all this?" they asked him.

"The king I served had an image of a hand," he answered. "The hand had five fingers, and on it were etched all the lines and creases found in the palm of a hand. This hand was in fact a map of all the worlds. On it was marked all that has been since heaven and earth were created and all that will be until the end. Everything in the world was marked on it, down to the last detail, in its lines and creases. It was like a map, and just as on a map there are letters by each mark to show that here is this city and there is that stream, so in the creases of the hand there were special symbols. Every country and city, every stream and river and mountain, in this world and in all the worlds, was marked out in its creases and lines. In the same way, each person in every country and all the events of their lives were marked on the hand.

"All the paths from one country to another and from one place to another were shown. That is how I knew how to enter this city, whose fortifications no man can pass. Were you to send me from this city to another, I would know the way. And just as the hand showed the paths between one city and another, it also marked those between the various worlds and those between heaven and earth. Elijah went up to heaven by one route, and it was marked there; Moses went up by another, and it too was marked; Enoch ascended by yet another, and that too was marked.

"Furthermore, everything was engraved on the hand as it was when the world was created, as it is now, and as it will be. Thus the city of Sodom appeared as it was before it was destroyed, while it was being destroyed, and after its destruction. Everything that ever was, is now, and ever will be was engraved on the hand. And on the hand I saw that the country whose people you say are all gods will be overthrown."

The people were amazed. What he was saying appeared to be true, for they knew that all things appear on a map of the world, and the lines of a hand look like letters. Furthermore, no man could invent such a story.

"Where is this king?" they asked the master of prayer. "Perhaps he will show us a way to find money."

"What, do you still want money?" he asked them in amazement. "Don't even speak of money!"

"Nevertheless, tell us where the king is," they begged him.

"I do not know where the king is," he answered. "This is what happened. Once there were a king and a queen, and they had an only daughter. When the time came for her to be wed, the king called a meeting of all his counselors, that they should advise him which man should be her husband. I, too, was one of the counselors, for the king loved me. I suggested that she be given to the warrior, for he had been of great help to us, and he had conquered many countries. It seemed fitting that the king's daughter be given to him as his wife. My advice was favored, and all agreed on it. There was great rejoicing at the court that a husband had been found for the king's daughter, and they were wed.

"The king's daughter bore a child. This child was wondrously beautiful; his beauty surpassed that of any mortal. His hair was of gold, and it shone with every color. His countenance was like the sun, and his eyes shone like the other heavenly lights. As soon as he was born, it was obvious that the child possessed great wisdom. When he heard people talking, he knew when to laugh and when to cry. It was plain that he understood what was being said, even though he did not yet know how to talk.

"There was a bard at the king's court, a master of rhetoric and verse. He knew how to speak very beautifully, and he composed exquisite speeches, verses, and praises for the king. This bard was very talented by nature, but the king showed him the source of his art, where he could obtain the power of speech, and he became a most wonderful bard.

"There was a sage, too, at the king's court. This sage was very wise by nature, but the king showed him where he could obtain wisdom, and he became even wiser.

"The warrior, too, was strong by nature, but the king showed him where to obtain power, and he became a great and terrible warrior.

"There is a sword which hangs in midair. This sword possesses three kinds of power. When it is raised, all the commanders of the opposing army run away, and the enemy is of course defeated, for there is no one left to conduct the war. But if the soldiers still desire to fight, the sword has two edges, and each of these has its own special power. One makes all the soldiers fall, and the other smites them with a withering of the flesh, may God protect us from it. A thrust of the sword with one edge or the other is all that is necessary to subdue the enemy. The king showed the warrior the way to the sword, and from there he derived his great might.

"The king also showed me the source of my power, from which I derive what I need.

"The king also had a faithful friend, who loved him with very great devotion. Their love for one another was so great that they could not bear to be parted even for an hour. And since there are times when men cannot be together, they had their portraits painted. They took great pleasure in gazing at these pictures whenever they were not together. The figures showed how much the king and his faithful friend loved one another, and how devotedly they embraced and kissed each other. The portraits had a special power, so that whoever looked at them was filled with great love. The king's friend, like the others, received the gift of love from the source that the king had shown him.

"One day, when everyone—the bard, the warrior, and all the members of the court—had each gone to the place the king had shown him to replenish his power, a great tempest arose, and it cast the whole world into confusion. The sea became dry land, and the dry land became sea; deserts became cities, and cities deserts. The tempest also reached the king's court. There it caused no damage, but it snatched away the child. In the midst of the panic, the king's daughter ran off after the child. After her ran the queen, and after the queen, the king, and all were scattered.

"At that time, none of us was there, for we had all gone to renew our powers. When we returned, we found that they had disappeared, and that the hand, too, was lost. Since that time, we have all been dispersed. We can no longer go each to his own place to renew his power, for since the world has been overturned, the roads have changed, and we do not know them. But though we can no longer go to the source of our power, the little that remains to each of us is still very great. And so if this warrior is the warrior who served the king, he is certainly very powerful."

The people listened to everything he said, and marveled greatly. They would not let him leave, in case the approaching warrior was really the one whom he knew.

Meanwhile the warrior was coming closer to the country and sending his messengers. Finally he reached its very borders and took up a position below the city, and he sent his emissaries from there. The people were terrified, and they begged the master of prayer to tell them what to do. "I must know more about this man," he told them, "to discover whether or not he is the king's warrior."

The master of prayer left the city and went to the warrior's camp. He started talking to one of the sentries. "What are you doing, and how did you come to join this warrior?" he asked him.

"I'll tell you how it came about," answered the man. "It is recorded in our chronicles that there was once a great tempest that overturned the entire world. The sea became dry land, and the dry land sea; deserts became cities, and cities deserts. Everything in the world was thrown into confusion.

"After the tempest had abated, the people of the world decided they wanted a king, and they began to search for someone who would be fitting to rule over them. They decided that the most important thing to be taken into consideration was the true purpose of life. Whosoever devoted the greatest efforts to attaining that goal would be worthy of being king.

"The people began to inquire into the nature of the true purpose of life, but because they had different opinions, they soon broke up into several sects.

"One sect maintained that the true purpose of life was honor. It is obvious, they said, that honor is the most important thing in the world, for impugning a man's honor is like shedding his blood. A man's honor is respected even after his death, and he is given an honorable burial. The dead have no need for money, for they desire nothing, but one is careful to protect their honor.

"By means of such arguments, the members of this sect reasoned that honor is the true purpose of life, and they decided to seek out a man of honor. A man who already commanded honor, and sought even more, and thereby strengthened the natural desire for honor—such a man was attaining the true purpose of life, and he would be worthy of being king.

"They went in search of such a person, and on their way they saw an old gypsy beggar being borne aloft, with about five hundred gypsies following in his wake. This beggar was blind, deformed, and dumb, and the people following him were his family. They were a large clan, a veritable multitude, and they bore him on their shoulders and carried him around. Now this old beggar was very careful of his honor! He was a most irascible old man, continually scolding his mob of followers and ordering that someone else carry him and frequently losing his temper. Clearly this old beggar was a person of tremendous honor. He already commanded honor, he sought more honor, and he protected his honor most carefully. He won great favor among the members of this sect, and they made him their king.

"Since the properties of a land are conducive to the development of particular attributes, the members of this sect looked for a country that would facilitate and foster the development of honor. They found such a country and settled there.

"Another sect maintained that honor is not the true purpose of life. They deliberated, and they concluded that it must be murder, for, as all can see, everything in the world is doomed to extinction. Plants, trees, and all that grows, men and everything that exists on earth, all must in the end cease to be. Death, apparently, is the ultimate purpose, and so a murderer who kills people and thereby puts an end to their existence brings the world closer to its goal. They concluded, therefore, that the true purpose of life is murder. A murderer, someone fierce and full of rage, was reaching this goal, and such a person would be worthy of being king.

"These people went in search of such a murderer, and on their way they heard a terrible cry. They inquired into its source and were told that someone had just killed his father and mother. 'Could there be a murderer more hardhearted and more fierce,' they exclaimed, 'than one who would murder his father and mother?' This man had attained the ultimate. He pleased them very much, and so they took him to be their king. Then they sought a country that would be suitable for murder. They chose a place in the mountains where many murderers dwelt, and went to live there with their king.

"Another sect said that the king should be someone who had a great abundance of food but did not eat what ordinary men eat, and subsisted on delicacies, such as milk, that do not coarsen the brain. As they could not find anyone who did not eat the food of ordinary men, they settled for the time being for a rich man who had a great abundance of food. He would be their king until they found the man they really wanted, at which time the rich man would be expected to abdicate. They made him their king, chose a country which was suited to their predilections, and settled down.

"Another sect maintained that they should be ruled by a beautiful woman. 'The true purpose of the human race,' they said, 'is to populate the world. It was for this reason that the world was created. Since beauty arouses desire, and desire brings about procreation, it clearly furthers the true purpose.' The members of this sect chose a beautiful woman, and she became their queen. They sought out a land that would be congenial to beauty and settled there.

"Another sect said that the true purpose is speech, for speech is what distinguishes man from beast and makes man the greater. Their goal was an orator who had mastered the art of speech, knew several languages, and could speak at all times. They went in search of someone who suited their ideal. Shortly they found a mad Frenchman who went around talking to himself. They asked him if he could speak any other languages, and he did know several. This man had surely attained the goal, for he was a master of rhetoric, knew several languages, and talked an enormous amount; he even talked to himself! He won their favor, and they made him their king. Having chosen a suitable country, they settled there with their king, and he surely led them along the straight path!

"Another faction said that the true purpose of life is merriment. One rejoices when a child is born, at weddings, and when one's own country conquers another. Evidently, merriment is the true purpose. Someone who is always merry would be fit to rule. So they set out to search for such a man. After a while they saw a fellow walking around, wearing a dirty shirt, and holding a bottle of spirits. He was accompanied by others like him. Now this fellow was very merry, because he was very drunk and had no worries. He pleased them greatly, for he had plainly reached the goal, so they made him king over them. He surely led them along the straight path! They chose a suitable country, where there were many vineyards. From the grapes they made wine, and they made liquor from the pips so that nothing would be wasted. They were always merry without knowing why and, in fact, for no reason.

"Another sect maintained that the true purpose of life was wisdom. They looked for a great sage and made him king. Then they sought out a country that was congenial to wisdom and settled there.

"Yet another sect maintained that the true purpose of life was to exercise, eat, and drink in order to build up the body. They looked for a muscular man who ate and drank and exercised a great deal to increase the size of his limbs. Someone who had a large body, they reasoned, had a bigger portion in the world, for he occupied more space. Such a man was close to the goal and therefore fit to be king. They found a large man whose well-developed body won their approval, and he became their king. They sought out a country suited to body building and settled there.

"And there was another sect which maintained that all these things were not the true purpose of life. The real goal, they believed, was to pray to God, of blessed Name, and to be humble and lowly. The members of this sect sought out a man of prayer and made him their king."

After the sentry had related all this to the master of prayer, he added that he and the fighting men who had joined up with the warrior were of the sect of the body builders; they had taken a strong man to be their king. One day a party of them had been traveling, together with wagons filled with provisions.

Everyone was terrified of these huge, powerful body builders and made sure to move out of their way. Then a powerful warrior approached them from the other direction. Not only did he not move aside, but he walked straight through their ranks, scattering them in all directions and eating all the provisions on the wagons. The fighting men were very frightened, and they were astonished that there was a warrior so great he had no fear of them. They immediately prostrated themselves before him and proclaimed: "Long live the king!" He certainly deserved to be king, according to their belief that the goal of life was to have a large body. So mighty and powerful of limb was the warrior that their reigning monarch would surely abdicate in his favor.

"And so it was," concluded the sentry. "We made him our king, and he is the warrior with whom we are conquering the world. But he tells us that the object of his campaign is not to subjugate the world. He has another purpose."

"What is the source of the warrior's power?" asked the master of prayer.

"When a country refuses to surrender itself to him," replied the sentry, "the warrior takes up his sword. This sword has three powers. When it is raised, all the enemy's commanders flee. . . ." And he described in detail the powers of the sword. When he heard this, the master of prayer was certain that their leader was none other than the king's warrior, and he asked whether he might see him. The sentry said that he had to ask permission, which the warrior gave.

As soon as the master of prayer came into the presence of the warrior, they recognized each other and rejoiced and wept. They rejoiced over the good fortune of their reunion, and they wept as they remembered the king and his companions. Then they recalled everything that had happened to them and how they came to be there.

The warrior told his story. After the great tempest he returned from the place where he had gone to renew his power and found that the king and all his court were gone. From then on he had wandered around the world. On his travels he had passed close to each of the king's counselors but had never been able to find them. Once, as he passed a particular place, he had realized that the king must surely be nearby, but he did not know exactly where. In another place, he was certain that the queen was nearby, but he could not find her either. In the same way he had passed close to all the other members of the king's court. "You are the only one I did not pass," he concluded.

"I, too, came across the places where they were dwelling," answered the master of prayer. "I passed close to where you were, too. In one place, I saw the king's crown. I knew that the king must be nearby, but I was unable to find him. Later I came upon a sea of blood, and I knew that it was from tears that the queen had shed over all that had happened, but I could not find her. Then I came upon a sea of milk, and I understood that it was from the breasts of the king's daughter, who could no longer nurse her child. She must have been nearby, but I could not find her. Then I saw some golden hairs lying on the ground, and I knew that they belonged to the child, but I did not take them. The child was certainly nearby, but I could not find him. Later I came upon a sea of wine, and I knew that it must have flowed from the words of consolation of the bard, who had tried to comfort the king and the queen and the king's daughter. I knew that he must be nearby, but I could not find him. Then I saw a stone on which the likeness of the hand had been carved, and I knew that the sage must have engraved it, but it was impossible to find him. Finally, on a mountain, I saw the king's golden tables and utensils, and his treasures, and I knew that the king's treasurer was close at hand, but it was impossible to find him."

"I, too, passed by all those places," the warrior said, "but I did take some of the child's golden hair. I took seven hairs, each of a different hue, and they are very precious to me. I settled in a certain place and lived on whatever came to hand, on grass and other plants. When there was nothing left to eat, I moved on, but I forgot my bow there."

"I saw the bow!" interrupted the master of prayer. "I knew that it must surely be yours, but I couldn't find you."

"When I left that place," the warrior continued, "I wandered around until one day I came upon a band of strong men. I was famished, and so I broke their ranks to find food. And then they made me a king! Now I am campaigning to conquer the world, but my true purpose is to find the king and all his companions."

The master of prayer began to speak with the warrior about the country of wealth, whose people had been so corrupted by the lust for money that they had fallen into the folly of believing that those who possess large amounts of money are gods. The warrior replied that the king had once told him that men can be extricated from any base desire except the love of money. "So," he continued, "you will not be able to sway them. The king told me that such men can only be freed by going along the road that leads to the sword from which I derive my power."

Thus they spoke together for a long time, and in the end the master of prayer persuaded the warrior to give the people more time. Then they agreed upon certain signs with which they would keep in touch with each other.

The master of prayer went on his way, and he encountered a group of people who were carrying prayerbooks and praying as they went. He was in awe of them, and they too were in awe of him. He stood to pray, and so did they. Then he asked them, "Who are you?"

"At the time of the great tempest," they answered, "all the people of the world were divided into sects, each of which chose a different way of life. We decided that the true purpose of life is to pray at all times to God. We sought and found a man of prayer, and we made him our king."

When the master of prayer heard this, he was overjoyed, for this was what he desired. He began to speak with them, and he revealed to them the way he prayed, and his books, and his other ways. When they heard his words, their eyes were opened, and they saw his greatness. They immediately made him their king, and their former king abdicated in his favor.

The master of prayer studied with his people. He opened their eyes and revealed to them how they ought to pray to God. They had been righteous before, since they had prayed at all times, but the master of prayer made them great saints. He sent a letter to the warrior, telling him of his good fortune in finding such people, who had made him their king.

Meanwhile, the people of the country of wealth carried on their folly and their rites, and the time that the warrior had granted them was running out. They were terrified, and they stepped up their rituals, offering sacrifices, burning incense, and devoting themselves to their prayers. Then they once again decided to send for help to the country whose inhabitants were as gods, being so very rich. They still believed that this country could save them.

So they sent messengers to this country, but these messengers lost their way and came upon a man walking along with a staff. Now this staff was inlaid with so many precious gems that it was worth more than the riches of all their gods put together. It was probably worth more than the riches of their own gods and of the gods of the country to which they were going, all added together. The man's hat was also inlaid with jewels, and it, too was exceedingly valuable. The messengers immediately fell down before him, bowing and prostrating themselves. According to their folly, his great wealth made this man a god above all gods.

In fact, he was the king's treasurer. "If you think that this is special," he said, "come with me, and I'll show you real riches!" He led them to the mountain and showed them the king's treasures. They immediately fell down again and bowed and prostrated themselves to this god of gods. However, they did not offer him any sacrifices. Since they thought that he was a great god, they would have liked to have sacrificed themselves to him, but they had been strictly forbidden to do this. Those who had dispatched them had been concerned that, were they to do so, none would reach the destination. One would find a treasure on the road, another would go to a water closet and find jewels there, and they would start sacrificing themselves until no one was left.

The messengers decided that there was no point in going on to the country to which they had been sent, because this man would doubtless be able to help them even more. Since they thought that he was a greater god than all the others, they begged him to return with them to their own country. He liked the idea and went with them. When they returned to their country, the people were overjoyed to have acquired such a great god. They had no doubt that he would be able to help them.

The king's treasurer, like all the counselors of the king's court, was in fact a righteous man. He was very pained by the foolish customs of the country, but he could not yet turn the people from their evil ways. Nevertheless, he issued a decree prohibiting all sacrifices until order was restored.

When they began to tell him about the warrior who was threatening the country, he, like the master of prayer, said, "Perhaps this is the warrior I once knew?" He left the city and went to the warrior's camp, and he asked one of the sentries whether he could see the warrior. The sentry went to ask permission, which the warrior gave. As soon as the treasurer went into the warrior's presence, they recognized each other and rejoiced and wept.

The warrior said, "Our worthy master of prayer was here, too, and he has become a king!"

The treasurer told him about all the places he had passed close to where the king and all his counselors had been, and how the master of prayer and the warrior were the only two he had not encountered. Then the two discussed the country whose people had sunk into folly and corruption because of their lust for money. The warrior told the treasurer, as he had the master of prayer, that the king had once told him that whosoever sank into the lust for money could not be freed of it except by going along the road that leads to the sword. The treasurer persuaded the warrior to grant them some more time. They agreed upon certain signs with which they could keep in touch with each other, and they parted.

When the treasurer returned to the country, he began to exhort the people, telling them how bad their path was, and that they had been led astray and corrupted by the lust for money. He could not move them, so deeply entrenched were they in their evil ways. Nevertheless, they had heard so many reproofs from the master of prayer, and now from the treasurer, too, that at last they said, "Very well then, if we are really in error, please free us of it." But they did not mean what they said and had no desire to abandon their folly.

"I can tell you what to do about the warrior," the treasurer told his people. "I know all about the warrior's strength and from where he derives his power." And he told them about the sword, the source of the warrior's power. "I can lead you to the place of the sword," he said. "By going there together, we shall be able to overcome him." In his heart, however, the treasurer really hoped that by going on the road that leads to the sword, they would be freed from their folly.

His advice was taken, and he set out with a group of their leaders on the road to the sword. These men, who were considered gods, adorned themselves with ornaments of gold and silver, that all might see their wealth.

The treasurer sent word to the warrior about his mission and his hope of finding the king and his counselors on the way.

The warrior answered that he wished to join them. He disguised himself, so that none but the treasurer would know who he was, and joined the company that was going to the place of the sword. Then they decided to tell the master of prayer as well, and he said that he would join the company. Before he set out, he bade his people to pray to God for the success of

their mission: that they would find the king and his companions. He had always prayed for this, and now he bade his
people to do the same. He had written special prayers for this.
The master of prayer joined the treasurer and the warrior, and
there was great joy at their reunion, rejoicing and weeping, as
on earlier occasions.

The three of them traveled for a long time, together with the
"gods" of the land of wealth, until they came to a certain country. They asked the guards stationed at the border, "What kind
of country is this, and who is your king?"

The guards answered that at the time of the great tempest,
when the people in the world were divided into sects, they had
decided that the true purpose of life was wisdom. They had
taken a great sage to be their king. Recently they had found
another, even greater sage, who was unique in the depth of his
wisdom. Their own king had abdicated, and they had made the
greater sage king.

"It sounds as if this is our own sage," the three travelers
agreed, and they asked if they could see this king. Permission
was granted, and as soon as they entered his presence, they saw
that he really was the king's sage. Then there was great rejoicing, but they also wept, because they did not know how to
find the king and his family.

They asked the sage what had happened to the hand. He
replied that it was in his possession, but since the great tempest
that had scattered them all, he had not wanted to look at it, for
it belonged to the king. Nevertheless, he had engraved a copy
of it on a stone, that he might make use of it in time of need.

Then he told them that after the great tempest he had wandered around, and on his travels he had come across the places
where all of the king's men, except the three who were with him
now, had been. He wandered until he found this country, whose
people had made him their king. For the present, he had to
govern them according to their own ideas of wisdom, until the

time would come when he would be able to guide them to the real truth.

The counselors discussed with the sage the country whose people had been led astray by money. "If we were cast out and scattered for no other reason than to restore that country to the path of truth, it would still have been worthwhile," they told each other. Each of the other sects had chosen its particular folly—this one honor, that one murder, and so on—and had been misled, and all had to be guided toward the real truth. Even the sect that pursued wisdom had not attained the true goal, for its ideas were secular and heretical. It was easier to free them from their folly than the others, but it was most difficult of all to move the people of the land of wealth from their wrong ways. The sage added that he, too, had heard from the king that it was possible to free a man from any folly except the lust for money and that the only release from this was by going along the road to the sword.

The sage decided to join their company, and the four of them set out, together with the "gods" of the country of wealth, and reached another land. "What kind of country is this, and who is your king?" they asked the sentries.

After the great tempest, they were told, the people of this country had agreed that the purpose of human life was speech. They had found an orator, a master of many tongues, and made him their king. But later they had come upon an even greater master of the art of language, both bard and orator. Their own king had abdicated in his favor, and they had made him their king.

"This must surely be the king's bard," the four counselors said, and they asked if they might see the king. Permission was granted, and when they came into his presence, they saw that he really was the king's bard. Their rejoicing was great, but they also wept for the lost king. The bard, too, joined their company, and they continued their search, hoping to find the others. They saw that God was indeed helping them, and they were finding more and more of their comrades. They ascribed their good fortune to the master of prayer by virtue of whose prayers the reunion was coming about.

They reached another country, and there, too, they asked, "What kind of country is this, and who is your king?"

The guards told them that they were of the sect that believed that the purpose of life was to be drunk and merry. They had searched for someone who was always happy, and they had appointed a drunkard to be their king. Later they had come upon a man sitting by a sea of wine, and he pleased them more. They thought that he must surely be a great drunkard, and they had made him their king.

The companions then asked to see the king, and permission was granted. When they entered the presence of this king, they saw that he was the king's friend, and the sea of wine by which he had been sitting had flowed from elegies of the bard. Here, too, there was great rejoicing and weeping, and the friend joined the company.

They reached another country and asked the guards, "Who is your king?"

The guards replied that their ruler was a very beautiful woman. The people of this country had agreed that the purpose of life was to populate the world and that beauty helped to fulfill this. At first some pretty woman had been their queen, but later they had come upon a woman of incomparable beauty, and they had made her queen.

The counselors realized that this queen must surely be the king's daughter, and asked to see her. Permission was granted, and when they came into her presence, they saw that she really was the king's daughter. The joy of the reunion cannot be imagined.

"How did you come to be here?" they asked her, and she told them that when the great tempest had snatched the precious child from its cradle, she had run after him in pursuit but had not been able to find him. Her grief was great, and her milk flowed and flowed, until it formed a sea. Later, the people of this country had found her and made her their queen.

The counselors' rejoicing was great, but they also wept bitterly over the missing child and over the king and the queen, of whom they had heard nothing. Now, however, this country had a king, for the daughter was reunited with her husband, the warrior.

The daughter asked the master of prayer to stay in her country for a while, in order to cleanse its people of their pollution. Since they regarded beauty as the ultimate goal, they had sunk into terrible debauchery. Furthermore, they had made their lechery into a religion.

Then the counselors set out in search of the others, and they reached another country. "Who is your king?" they asked, and they were told that he was a one-year-old. The people of this country were of the sect that had decided that their king should be a man who had a great amount of food, but not the food of ordinary men. They had made a certain rich man their king, but then they had come upon someone sitting by a sea of milk. He pleased them very much, for all his life he had fed only on milk, and he had never eaten the food of ordinary men. They made him their king, and because he lived on milk like an infant, they called him a one-year-old.

The counselors realized that this king must be the lost child, and they asked to see him. Permission was granted, and when they came into his presence, they saw that he really was the child. He recognized them, too. Though he had been only an infant when he was snatched away, he had possessed such extraordinary wisdom even at birth that he remembered them. There was great rejoicing at that reunion, but they also wept, for they still knew nothing of the whereabouts of the king and queen.

"How did you come to be here?" they asked the child.

He told them that after the great tempest had snatched him

away, it had dropped him at a certain place, where he had lived on whatever he could find. Eventually he had come upon the sea of milk, which he understood must have flowed from his grief-stricken mother's breasts. He had stayed there, living on the milk, and then the people of this country had found him and made him their king.

They set out again, and then they reached another country. "Who is your king?" they asked, and they were told that these people were of the sect that had chosen murder as the ultimate goal. At first, a certain cutthroat had been their king, but later they had found a woman sitting by a sea of blood. They decided that she must be a great murderer, and they made her their ruler. The counselors asked to see her, and permission was granted. When they came into her presence, they saw that she was the queen, who had wept until her flowing tears had made a sea of blood. There was great rejoicing at the reunion, but weeping too, for they still knew nothing of what had become of the king.

They reached another country. "Who is your king?" they asked.

The people answered that since they thought that the true purpose of life was honor, they had chosen a very honored man as their king. Later they had come upon an old man sitting in a field wearing a crown. He must be a very honored person, they decided, for even when sitting in a field he still wore a crown. And they made him their king.

The counselors realized that this man must be their own king, and they asked to see him. Permission was granted, and when they entered his throne room, they recognized him. The human mind cannot possibly imagine the joy of that reunion. However, the foolish "gods" who had been traveling with the counselors had no idea why everyone was so happy.

Now that the holy company, the king and all the members of his court, was complete, the master of prayer was sent out to all the countries to correct them, to purify them, and to bring them out of their folly. He had the power to do this, for the other kings had conferred their authority upon him.

The warrior talked with the king about the country whose people had fallen so deeply into the idolatrous worship of money. "You once told me," he said, "that men can only be released from the lust for money by taking the road to the sword."

"Indeed, that is true," said the king. "On the road to the sword, there is a side path that leads to a mountain of fire. On that mountain crouches a lion that, when it is hungry, goes out and preys on flocks and devours sheep and cattle. He takes no heed of the shepherds, who make much noise and throw stones at him. The mountain of fire is quite invisible.

"Another side path leads from the road to the sword and reaches a place called the kitchen. Here there are many kinds of food, but no fire. The foods are cooked by means of pipes and channels from the mountain of fire, which is quite a long way from there. The kitchen also cannot be seen from the road, but it can be detected by the birds that hover over it. By the flapping of their wings, these birds can stir up the fire or quench it. They keep the flames at the proper heat for each of the different dishes.

"Go, then, and lead the people of the country of wealth to the kitchen. Make sure that they walk against the wind, and that the smells of the foods reach their nostrils. When you give them that food to eat, they will cast off their lust for money."

The warrior did as he was bid. He took the leaders of the country of wealth, all of whom were regarded as gods in their own country, and brought them along the road. Before these leaders had left their country with the treasurer, those who remained undertook to accept whatever was done in their name. The warrior led them along the road to the sword and up the side path to the kitchen. At first he took them against the wind, and the odor of the foods reached their nostrils. They pleaded with him to let them eat these delicacies. Then he turned them about and took them parallel to the wind, and they cried out, "What a dreadful stench!" He turned them around several times, and each time they begged for food or complained of the stench.

"Do you not see there is nothing here that smells bad?" the warrior said. "It can only be you, yourselves."

Then he took them to the kitchen and gave them food. As soon as they had eaten, they began to throw their money away, for they realized that it was the source of the stench. It stank like excrement. They were deeply ashamed, and each dug a pit and buried himself in it. In that place money was the most disgraceful of things, and the greatest insult one could hurl at someone was "You have money!" Whosoever had more money, his shame was the greater. None of the leaders of the country of wealth would show his face to his companions, much less to the warrior. Whosoever found that he still had a coin, even if it was just a penny, destroyed it or threw it away.

Then the warrior came and raised them out of the pits. "Come with me," he said. "You no longer need fear the warrior, for I am he."

The leaders asked him to let them take some of the foodstuffs back to their country. They themselves already found money revolting, and now they wanted their whole country to be freed from the lust for money. It was the special quality of these foods, that whosoever ate of them found money revolting.

So the warrior granted their wish, and they brought the food back to their country. As soon as their countrymen tasted it, they, too, immediately began to throw away their money and to bury themselves in the earth in great shame. The wealthiest people and the "gods" felt the greatest shame, but the lowly people, the beasts and the birds, were also ashamed to have considered themselves worthless just because they possessed no money. The people threw away all their money, their gold, and their silver, and they sent for the master of prayer, who gave them penances and told them how to correct their ways and purified them.

And the king ruled over the whole world, and all men turned to God, blessed is He, dedicating themselves to Torah, prayer, repentance, and good deeds. Amen. May this be His will.

Commentary

"The Master of Prayer" is perhaps the most original and highly polished of all Nachman's tales. Structurally it is made up of two major narrative frameworks, each with its central theme, and incorporates numerous short stories and fragments. The various characters, ideas, and allusions are integrated into an extremely rich yet remarkably uniform symbolic scheme. There is a highly detailed kabbalistic imagery, and there are literally hundreds of allusions drawn from the whole of Jewish literature, but especially from chapters 3 and 31 of the book of Isaiah.

This tale is also unique in its extensive use of humor. Nachman is occasionally very witty in his other stories, but here he employs humor in a wide variety of forms, from lighthearted jokes at the expense of various philosophical ideas and systems to the almost Swiftian satire of the country of wealth.

A single motif informs the whole tale—the redemption of the world in messianic times. Each of the two major narrative elements relates to this topic, though they start at different points in time and thus discuss it from different aspects. The first narrative, the story of the master of prayer and the country of wealth, starts in the present and deals more with human behavior; whereas the second, the history of the king's court and his counselors, begins with the creation of the world, and its concern is more theological. The two narrative elements merge together toward the end of the story.

THE MASTER OF PRAYER
AND THE LAND OF WEALTH

The master of prayer is clearly identifiable as a *zaddik*, a hasidic leader, but of a kind different from that portrayed in the story that follows "The Clever Man and the Simple Man." Typologically he is closer to what Nachman called the "*zaddik* of the generation"—that is, the spiritual leader who would appear in messianic times. Various other models can be detected in the personality of the master of prayer. One is the prophet Elijah, especially as he is described in texts that cast him as the precursor of the Messiah, and another is the Baal Shem Tov, Nachman's own great-grandfather. Nachman regarded the Baal Shem Tov as an example of the perfect *zaddik,* and he sought to emulate him in his own life.

Like the Baal Shem Tov, the master of prayer lives far from human habitation. Symbolically he has removed himself from "settled" people, whose modes of thought and of life prevent them from relating to truly significant concerns. His incursions into the towns are made solely to fulfill his task as a *zaddik,* to draw people to him, to "unsettle" them. He resembles the hasidic *zaddik* in other ways, too. The technique he employs to guide his followers on the path to spiritual perfection—prescribing individual remedies for different souls, generally based on their previous way of life—is one that was frequently adopted by the great masters. Furthermore, though he is other-worldly, when necessary he can outwit his worldly adversaries in their own territory, as when he eludes those who are search-ing for him.

In his treatment of the country of wealth, Nachman shows himself to be a master of literary satire. He starts by describing a situation that, while strange in certain features, is nevertheless plausible and recognizable. However, as he fills in more details about the situation and the way it develops, a picture emerges of a society that is both monstrous and absurd. The strength of the satire and the power of its message lie in the consistency of its internal logic. In this property-oriented state, the mad out-come is not the result of a moment's insanity but is the natural and inevitable consequence of the people's loyalty to their principles.

Although in certain features (for example, pennants as a means of denoting social rank) the country of wealth resembles ancient Rome, on the whole the description is that of a modern society, and Nachman is clearly warning his contemporaries about the dangers of abandoning traditional values in favor of materialism. The difference between the inhabitants of the country of wealth and "real" people lies mainly in the stripping away of hypocrisy. In establishing a social stratification that ranks paupers as mere animals, the people of the country of wealth may seem to be extending their sacred principle to absurdity, but in fact it takes no great stretch of the imagination to see in this a reflection of contemporary society.

However, Nachman is concerned here with more than social criticism. The master of prayer knows that such a society will inexorably move in the direction of dehumanization and idolatry. The ideas espoused by its people have a momentum of their own. Thus the ancient and "respectable" belief that the ores of precious metals found in the earth are created by the influence of the stars is developed in the country of wealth to its logical extreme; and, first, wealth and, then, the possessors of wealth are *equated* with stars. This species of faulty reasoning, which derives from identifying those fragments of reality that most interest man with the essence of all existence, lies at the root of all idolatry (and frequently of heretical deviations from true religion as well). From here the step to human sacrifice is short.

When the master of prayer sets out to save the country of wealth, he does so like a true hasidic *zaddik*. He begins his work among the humble—in this case, the watchmen whose status is so low that they are permitted to breathe the same air as ordinary mortals. The fact that he fails to move even these unfortunate folk, who are victims of the system they espouse, shows that no persuasion, no logic, can dislodge the country of wealth from its folly. Nachman has described such situations in a number of tales, and the solution is always the same: an external force is required. The agent of change in this story is the threat posed by the warrior.

The crisis created by the approach of an invincible army is utilized by the master of prayer in his second visit to the country, and on this occasion his spiritual inquisition of the poor is partially successful. When it comes to the rich and powerful, however, he can gain their attention only by relating to their own utilitarian interest. By indicating that he knows the warrior, he allows them to think that he may be able to intercede for them and save them from having to give up their wealth, and that later they may derive material benefit from finding the king or reading the hand.

THE HAND AND THE ROYAL COURT

The second major narrative element, which is introduced at this point, is characterized by an extensive use of kabbalistic symbolism. Indeed, it can be seen as a mystical allegory of the entire history of the world, from Creation through Redemption. Several of the images are familiar from other stories, though they are given in greater detail here; others appear in this story for the first time.

The image of the Torah—the hand, whose five fingers parallel its five books—as a map of all facets of existence is an ancient idea. It has roots in the Bible and the Midrash, where it is said that God used the Torah as a blueprint for creation. In the Kabbalah this concept deepened, and the Torah came to be perceived as a key to all the worlds. Thus, by studying the Torah, man could glimpse the totality of existence and even use it as a guide in his ascent to the heavens.

The ten members of the court—the royal family and the counselors—are at one level symbolic of the ten *Sefirot,* the manifestations of the Divine according to the Kabbalah. At another level the king's counselors represent specific biblical personalities and individual great men of all times; as such, they are the eternal personifications—and the highest degree of perfection—of particular qualities or attributes.

The king, as in other stories, is God, and the king's daughter is the *Shekhinah.* The warrior, to whom she is wed, is the man who fights for God and strives to subdue His enemies both in the world and in men's souls. It is written in the Zohar, the great work of Jewish mysticism, that whosoever overcomes his own nature receives the king's daughter. On a more historic level, the warrior is a kind of perfect *zaddik* and simultaneously a symbolic representation of the Messiah, son of Joseph, the precursor of the final Messiah, son of David; his task is to subdue the world and to bring it to the worship of God.

The infant is clearly the Messiah, son of David, and the description given here, of a person who embodies all virtues and perfections even from his birth, is derived from the book of Isaiah and the Zohar.

The king directs each of his counselors to a source to which he must go periodically in order to replenish his special power.

When all the counselors are absent at once for this purpose, the structure of the court is weakened, and the tempest—always a symbol of the power of evil—disrupts the world and overturns its order. This beautifully written account is in fact a literary rendering of the kabbalistic understanding of the Creation. The primal harmony that once existed was shattered in the cataclysmic event known as the "Breaking of the Vessels"; and as a result sparks of holiness were dispersed throughout the world. The task of man is to find and raise these sparks and to restore order to the cosmos. However, the task is extremely difficult— the king is not to be found, the *Shekhinah* is in exile, and the primal Torah now exists only as a memory. In such a state most men fall into despair: the counselors, on the other hand, are still motivated by their loyalty to their king and their hope for restitution. There is no longer any communication with God, but the memory of their wondrous companionship is enough to maintain them indefinitely in the fallen world. This concept of the "residue" of a now-vanished closeness to God is central to Nachman's theology.

THE SECTS AND THE COMPANIONS

After the dispersion mankind had no contact with God. However, the basic urge to seek for divinity still existed; and in the story it is translated into the search for perfection. The emergence of the various cults reflects the fact that a human being cannot relate to the totality of existence and must channel and direct his energy in accordance with the dictates of his religious personality. The cults are, in fact, basic human types; each is characterized by an attribute that is possessed in perfect form by one of the king's counselors or a member of his family. What

Nachman is attacking so ferociously in this section is not the actual activity of searching but the way that this quest can be perverted and debased. The "kings" who so degrade it are manifestations of human folly in its extreme.

There is a remarkable similarity between the higher and the debased forms of the various attributes, despite their polar differences. Thus, in one sect, the glory of the king, or God, is translated into the inane pursuit of honor. In another, the divine power of restriction, of discrimination, and of death that makes possible further life (represented by the queen) becomes, in its perverted form, the sect of murderers: necessary death becomes wanton killing. It should be noted that in Nachman's brilliant cataloging of the various follies of mankind, two of the sects receive scant treatment. The shortcomings of cleverness are well covered in "The Clever Man and the Simple Man," and apparently prayer was never debased.

The following table presents in schematic form the relationships between the members of the king's court and the perverted and higher forms of each attribute:

Member of Court	Representative of:	Debased Virtue	Higher Virtue
King	God	Honor	Glory
Queen	———	Destruction, murder	Understanding, analytic power
King's daughter	*Shekhinah*	Orgiastic fecundity	Divine abundance
Warrior	Precursor of Messiah	Physical prowess	Spiritual prowess
Lover	Abraham	Drunkenness	Unlimited love
Sage	Moses	Cleverness	Torah, wisdom

Member of Court	Representative of:	Debased Virtue	Higher Virtue
Treasurer	Aaron, high priest	Wealth	Blessing
Bard	King David, Levites	Verbosity, prolixity	Praise of God
Infant	Messiah	Health, care of body	Perfection
Master of prayer	Elijah, *zaddik* of the generation	Prayer (not debased)	Prayer

THE BEGINNING OF THE RESTITUTION

The process of restoring the world to its primal harmony must have a number of stages. First, the counselors and their respective sects must find each other, and the relationship of king and his subjects has to be established. As kings, the counselors will be able to fulfill their cosmic task in bringing about the Redemption. At this point the sects are drawn to the counselors because they see in them manifestations of the perfection they seek, but they still cannot distinguish between its noble and its base forms. The counselors, too, are still unable to raise the people from idolatry and can do no more than eliminate the worst abuses and excesses. The complete reform of mankind can come about only when all members of the royal court and the counselors are reunited, and the divine influence pervades all levels of existence.

It is important to note that the counselors seek not to suppress their peoples' debased attributes but to redirect those attributes to their proper goal. Here Nachman is expressing a basic concept of hasidic thought, that of "raising the sparks of holiness" that exist even in human vices. This is a form of sublimation: the correct way to overcome one's evil inclinations is not to suppress them but to redirect them from the base to the divine.

The search for the members of the king's family and the counselors is made easier by the various signs that each had left indicating that though they were inaccessible they still existed, and some residue of their former power was still present in the world. Thus the king's crown was to be seen—meaning that though God is not visible, His glory is still manifest. The sea of milk is the divine abundance that man can perceive but not enjoy.

The warrior and the master of prayer are the two principal architects of the restitution: the one on the organizational, physical level, the other on the spiritual. Neither can bring about the Redemption alone. Although the master of prayer is at a higher spiritual level than the warrior, he is essentially a solitary man and is most effective in dealing with individuals. Even his being appointed king of his sect does not change this: he gives his new followers spiritual knowledge, and this pleases him, but he remains alone.

The people of the country of wealth are a major stumbling block in the process of redemption. They are the only sect who have not installed one of the counselors as king, and they have to be brought into contact with the treasurer (who enters the story at a very late stage). However, even when all the members of the royal family and the companions are reunited with the king, and the other sects are ready to submit to his will, these worshipers of mammon are still unwilling to abandon their folly. The power of their vice is enormous. It encompasses all aspects of their existence, to the exclusion of every decent emotion. Earning money is an activity that can involve almost all of one's waking hours, enslaving all one's thoughts and acts. It is the only vice that cannot be sublimated or raised, and it must be broken from without. The people of the country of wealth must be led along the road to the sword to be purged. The source from which the warrior's sword derives its nourishment is fire so fierce that in it all passions are consumed.

THE CONCLUSION

The road to the sword is described in extremely dramatic and richly symbolic language, which is derived in part from chapter 31 of the book of Isaiah, but it is also replete with kabbalistic imagery. A dominant force here is the divine attribute of stern justice, that part of God's activity that punishes by destroying. In the normal course of events this attribute is not manifest in the world; and when it does appear, it does so suddenly, striking people like the lion who snatches sheep, despite the care of their spiritual leaders, the shepherds.

The mountain of fire is the manifestation of divine judgment in its most severe form: it consumes everything. However, it can be mitigated, and paths lead from the mountain to a place where the flames become a constructive force. Thus in the kitchen the fire consumes evil, but it also extracts and prepares nourishment for the world, turning bitter into sweet. In this it is assisted by the birds, who represent human souls. It is here, where hell fire is moderated, that the inhabitants of the country of wealth are purged of their depravity in a conclusion that is both pious and hilarious. When this happens, the primal harmony of the world is restored.

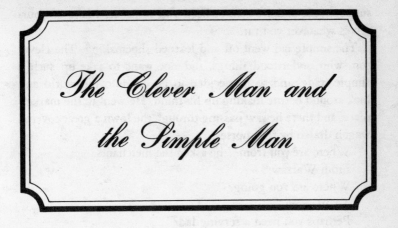

The Clever Man and the Simple Man

ONCE there were two householders who lived in the same town. Both of them were very wealthy, and they owned great houses.

Each of these householders had an only son, and the two children studied together in the same class. One of them was clever, and the other was simple; he was not stupid, but he had a plain mind, not subtle. Despite their different natures, the two children loved each other dearly.

After a number of years, the two householders began to lose their money. They sank lower and lower, until finally they lost almost everything. They became very poor and had nothing left but the houses in which they lived. The children were growing up, and their fathers told them, "We are no longer able to

support you, and we cannot keep you at home. Make of yourselves whatever you can."

The simple lad went off and learned shoemaking. The clever
son, who understood things, did not want to take up such a
simple trade, and so he decided to go out into the world and
look around before making up his mind. He went to the marketplace, and there he saw passing through the town a great covered
wagon drawn by four horses.

"Where are you from?" he asked the merchants.

"From Warsaw."

"Where are you going?"

"To Warsaw."

"Perhaps you need a serving lad?"

The merchants saw that he was clever and quick, and he
caught their fancy. They took him with them, and he served
them diligently along the way.

They arrived in Warsaw. Since he was a clever fellow, he
said to himself, "Now that I am here, why should I stay with
these merchants? Perhaps I can better myself elsewhere. I shall
look around and inquire."

He went to the marketplace and asked about the people who
had brought him and about his chances of finding a better
position. People answered him that the merchants who had
brought him were honest people and good employers, but that
working for them was difficult, because their business took them
to distant lands.

As he walked around the marketplace, the youth saw shop-
keepers' servants going about their business. He noticed their
fine manners, their fancy hats, and their pointed shoes. He was
a sharp and an understanding lad, and he liked the idea of
doing such work, both because of its elegance and because one
could do it without traveling. He returned to the merchants who
had brought him, thanked them, and told them that he did not
want to stay with them, and as for their having brought him to
Warsaw, he had already repaid them with his service on the

journey. He left them and found employment in the service of a shopkeeper.

The position of a servant is determined thus: at first he is an underservant and has to do heavy work for little pay, and only after some time can he rise to a higher position. This shopkeeper made the lad work hard. He would send him to the homes of the gentry to deliver merchandise, and the youth strained his arms, as servants do, carrying the heavy loads of cloth. Sometimes he had to carry merchandise up several flights of stairs. As he was a philosopher and understood things, he said to himself, "What's the point of my working like this? After all, the main reason a man works is to be able to marry and make a living, but I don't have to think about that yet. Meanwhile I can better myself by traveling around the world and seeing different countries."

The youth went to the marketplace, and there he saw a group of merchants traveling in a large wagon.

"Where are you going?" he asked them.

"To Livorno."

"Will you take me there, too?"

"Yes," they answered, and they took him to Livorno. From there he journeyed through Italy, and from Italy he went on to Spain.

His wanderings took him to many different countries, and this made him even more wise. After several years he said to himself, "Now the time has come to decide what I'm going to do with my life." He began to think philosophically about the profession he should take up. He liked the idea of being a goldsmith, for this is a great and beautiful craft and entails much wisdom as well. Furthermore, it promises a good living. He apprenticed himself to a goldsmith, and since he was sharp-witted and a philosopher, he mastered the trade in three months, though usually this takes several years. He became a master craftsman, and his skills surpassed even those of the goldsmith who had taught him. Once he had accomplished this, however, he said to himself, "Even though I have this trade in my hand, it's not enough. One can make a good living from it now, but that can change." So he apprenticed himself to a cutter of precious stones, and since he was so clever, he mastered this craft, too, in a short time, about three months.

Thereafter he reflected philosophically, "I have mastered these two trades, but, who knows, perhaps someday neither of them will be required. It would be prudent to study a profession that will always be needed." Deliberating with all his understanding and philosophy, he decided to study medicine, which is always needed and important.

In order to study medicine, one must first learn Latin, both to read and to write it, and philosophy as well. Since he was so clever, he learned all this in a short time, just three months. He became a great physician and philosopher, a master of all the sciences.

After a while, he began to find the whole world worthless. He was so clever, so skilled a craftsman, so wise a sage, and so great a physician, that everybody else in the world seemed of no account.

He then decided that it was time for him to settle down and take a wife. "But if I get married here," he thought, "who will notice? I shall return home, so that people will see what has become of me. When I left I was just a boy, and now I have attained greatness."

He set out on his way home. He suffered much on the journey. Because he was so wise there was no one with whom he could converse, and he could never find an inn to his liking. He was constantly suffering.

Let us now put aside the story of the clever man and begin to tell the story of the simple man.

The simple man learned shoemaking. Since he was simple, it took him a long time to acquire the skill, and even then he did not master it entirely. He took a wife and made a living by his trade.

Since he was a simple man and was not skilled at his craft, he earned his living with great difficulty. He had to work all the time and had no time even to eat. He would snatch bites of bread as he sat over his leather, piercing holes with his awl and sewing the heavy stitches.

The simple man lived in great happiness. He knew nothing but joy. He had every kind of food and drink and clothing that he desired. "My wife," he would say, "bring me something to eat." She would give him a piece of bread. When he had finished eating it, he would say, "Bring me some chicken soup with kasha." She would cut him another slice of bread, and he would eat it, praising its fine taste. "How delicious and satisfying this soup is," he would say. Then he would tell her, "Bring me some meat." Again she would give him bread, and as he ate it he would enjoy it and praise it handsomely. "This meat is delicious!" he would exclaim. Every time he asked her to bring him a fine dish, she would give him a piece of bread. He would enjoy it immensely, praise its quality, and talk about how delicious it was, exactly as though he were really eating the fine dish he had asked for. Because of his great innocence and happiness, he actually tasted in the bread he ate the flavor of any food he desired.

After the meal, when he said, "My wife, bring me a drink of beer," she would bring him a glass of water. "How delicious this beer is," he would exclaim. Next he would say, "Bring me some mead." She would give him more water, and he would praise the fine quality of the mead. "Bring me wine," he would demand, or perhaps he wanted some other beverage—whatever it was, she always gave him water, and he would enjoy and praise it exactly as if he were really drinking the beverage he had requested.

And so it was with clothing. He and his wife had but a single sheepskin coat between them. Whenever he needed the sheepskin to go to market, he would say, "My wife, give me the sheepskin," and she would give it to him. When he went visiting and needed a cloth coat, he would say, "My wife, give me the cloth coat." She would give him the sheepskin. In delight he would exclaim, "What a well-made cloth coat this is!" To go to the synagogue, he needed a caftan. "My wife, give me the caftan!" he would say, and she would give him the sheepskin. "How fine and how beautiful this caftan is!" he would declare. Sometimes, too, he had occasion to wear a fur coat. His wife would give him the sheepskin, and he would praise it, taking pleasure in the fine quality and beauty of his fur coat.

He did the same with all things, and so he was always filled with joy and happiness.

As he was not a master of his craft, it sometimes happened that when he finished a shoe it had three points instead of two. He would take the shoe in his hand, praise it highly, and take great pleasure in beholding it. "My wife," he would say, "how pretty and fine this shoe is, and how sweet. It is a shoe of honey and sugar."

"If that is really so," she would answer, "why do the other cobblers take three kopecks for a pair of shoes, and you take only a kopeck and a half?"

"What does that matter to me? What they do is their business, and what I do is my business. Anyway, why should we talk about what other people do? Let's reckon up how much profit I make on this shoe. The leather costs so much, the glue and the thread so much, and all the other materials so much. So altogether I earn ten pennies. But what does it matter to me if I make so much profit?"

So the simple man was always happy and cheerful. However, everybody used to mock him. He was just what they needed, a butt for their jokes. People considered him a lunatic. They used to come and start conversations with him in order to make fun of him. "No fooling, please," the simple man would tell them. If someone answered, "No fooling," he would listen and talk with him seriously. He did not want to think deeply and to wonder whether this answer itself was a joke. If, however, he saw that someone was really bent on making fun of him, he would say, "What if you are more clever than I am? That only makes you a fool. After all, what am I? If you are just more clever than I am, you are really a fool."

Meanwhile, the news that the clever man was coming and that he had become a very great and wise man caused a stir in the town. The simple man, too, went running joyously to greet him. "Quickly!" he said to his wife. "Give me the fur coat. I am going to meet my beloved friend; I'll see him at long last!" She gave him the sheepskin, and he rushed off to meet the clever man as he rode up in grand style in his carriage.

The simple man greeted him with great joy and affection. "My dear brother, how are you? Blessed be God who has brought you here and allowed me to see you."

The clever man looked at him. As the whole world was as nothing to him, he could not see much in this man, who looked like a lunatic. Nevertheless, because of the great love they had had for each other as youths, he took him into his carriage and rode with him into town.

Meanwhile, the two householders had died, and they had left their houses to their sons. Because the simple man lived nearby, he had entered his father's house and taken his inheritance. The clever man, however, had been away in foreign lands. There had been no one to take possession of his house, and it had fallen into decay and ruin. By now nothing remained of it, so on his return he had nowhere to live. He went to stay at an inn, but it was not to his liking, and he suffered there a great deal.

The simple man now had a new pastime: he began to visit the clever man frequently, always in a mood of affection and joy. He soon saw that his friend was suffering at the inn. "My brother," he said, "come to stay with me at my house. I will gather all my things into one corner, and my whole house will be at your disposal." The suggestion appealed to the clever man, and he came to stay with the simple man.

The clever man suffered all the time. It became known that he was a very wise man, an artist and a craftsman and a great physician. One day, a nobleman came by and asked him to make a gold ring. He prepared a most exquisite ring, cutting the designs with great skill and engraving on it a wonderful tree. However, when the nobleman returned, he did not like the ring. The clever man suffered terribly from this. He knew that in Spain this ring, engraved with the image of such a tree, would be highly regarded; here, however, there was nobody who could appreciate it. On another occasion a great nobleman arrived, bringing with him a precious jewel imported from some distant land. He had another jewel with an engraving on it, and he commissioned the clever man to copy this design onto the first jewel. The clever man made an accurate imitation which greatly pleased the nobleman. The clever man knew, however, that his work was flawed and that he had made a minute error that no one but he himself could notice. This, too, caused him great suffering. "Even though I am so clever," he said to himself, "I can still make mistakes."

His work as a physician was also a source of suffering. One day he visited a sick man and gave him a remedy. He knew that the patient's only chance of recovering was to take this potent draft. But the man died nevertheless, and everyone said that it was his fault. He suffered greatly from this. On the other hand, if a patient he had treated did recover, everyone said that it had happened by chance. He was always suffering.

When he needed some new clothes, the clever man went to the tailor and explained at great length exactly how he wanted the garment to be sewn. The tailor did as he was told, but he made a small error, and so one of the lapels turned out crooked. This, too, upset the clever man. "Here no one will notice anything," he said to himself, "but if I were in Spain with this lapel, I would be a laughingstock." He was always suffering.

The simple man was always running, happy and content, to his clever friend. Finding him sorrowful and suffering, he asked him, "As wise and as wealthy as you are, why are you always suffering? And why am I always so happy?"

The clever man was amused to hear such words from someone he deemed a lunatic. The simple man noticed this, and he continued, "Ordinary people are no more than fools when they mock me. Even though they're smarter than I am, that doesn't make them more than fools. How much more does this apply to a clever man like you! What's the point of showing that you're more clever than I am?

"How much better it would be," the simple man suddenly exclaimed, "if you were to become like me!"

"It is indeed possible that I could become like you," replied the clever man. "If God were to take away my reason, or if I were to fall ill and go mad, I could indeed become a lunatic like you. But you couldn't possibly become like me. You could never become as wise and clever as I am."

"For God, everything is possible," answered the simple man. "I could attain your wisdom in the twinkling of an eye."

At this, the clever man laughed heartily.

The two sons were known to everybody by the names "Clever" and "Simple." There are any number of clever people and simple people in the world, but these two were exceptional, for they both were from the same town and had studied together in the same class, and the one had become so extremely wise and the other so utterly simple. Even in the official register of the country, where everyone's name is recorded, these two sons were listed as "Clever" and "Simple."

Once the king happened to peruse this register, and he was surprised that two people should have names like "Clever" and "Simple," and he wanted to see the men who bore them. "But if

I just summon them to appear before me," thought the king, "they will be frightened. The clever man won't be able to speak his mind, and the simple man may well go mad with fright." The king decided, therefore, to send a clever messenger to the clever man and a simple messenger to the simple man. But how does one find a simple man in the royal capital, where all the people are generally so clever? There is always at least one simple man in the city, the king's treasurer. It is not desirable to make a clever man treasurer, because, being clever, he is likely to squander the country's wealth, and so a simple man is generally chosen for this task. The king called for a clever man and for the simple treasurer and charged them to send for the two sons. He prepared letters addressed to each and also sent a note to the governor of the province in which the two sons resided. In this note he commanded the governor to send letters to the two men in his own name, so that they would not be frightened. The king told him to write that the matter was not urgent. The king was not insisting that they come; it was up to them to choose. They could do as they liked, but the king would like to see them.

The two messengers set out and traveled to the governor's residence. On their arrival, they gave the governor the note addressed to him. He read it, and he then asked them about the two sons. They told him that the clever man was extraordinarily brilliant and was also very wealthy, while the simple man was indeed simple and had one sheepskin which was, to him, every kind of clothing. The governor decided that it would not be appropriate for the simple man to appear before the king in a sheepskin, so he had some more suitable clothes made, and he put them in the simple messenger's carriage. Then he gave the messengers the letters the king had requested, and they set off on their journey once again.

The messengers arrived at the home of the two sons and delivered the letters, the clever messenger to the clever man and the simple messenger to the simple man.

As soon as he was given the letter, the simple man told the simple messenger, "I cannot read what's written here. Read it to me."

"I'll tell you in short what it says," answered the messenger. "The king wants you to come to him."

"You're not fooling?"

"It's absolutely true; no fooling at all."

The simple man was immediately filled with joy. He ran to tell his wife, "My wife, the king has sent for me!"

"Whatever for?" she asked. "Why has he sent for you?"

He had no time to answer her, for he rushed out happily and got straight into the carriage to go with the messenger. When he climbed inside, he saw the clothes the governor had prepared for him, and he was even happier. Now he had clothes, too. He was overjoyed.

Meanwhile the king received word that the governor had been acting improperly, and he dismissed him from his office. "It would be good," thought the king, "if an ordinary person, a simple man, were to be governor. A simple man would rule the country truthfully and honestly, because he knows nothing of subtleties and deceit."

So the king issued an order appointing as the new governor the simple man whom he had summoned. Since the simple man had to travel through the capital city of the province, guards were to be posted at the gates of the city to stop him as soon as he arrived and give him the official letter of appointment.

As the king had commanded, so it was done. The gates were manned, and as soon as the simple man arrived, he was stopped and told that he had been made governor.

"No fooling?" he asked.

"Of course not," they answered him. "No fooling."

The simple man immediately became governor and ruled with power and might.

Now fortune had raised him up, and since fortune makes wise, he gained a little more understanding. However, he did not use his new-found cleverness, and he conducted himself as simply as before. He governed the country with sincerity and truth and with decency, and he never acted dishonestly toward anyone. Indeed, to govern a country one needs no great intelligence or wit, only honesty and straightforwardness. When the people came before him for judgment, he would say, "You are innocent, and you are guilty." His decisions were guided by his straightforward grasp of the truth, with no guile or deception. He governed honestly, and he was much loved among the people.

The simple man had faithful advisors who were sincerely devoted to him. One of them, out of love for him, gave him some advice: "You know that one day you will have to appear before the king, for he has already summoned you. Furthermore, even in the ordinary course of things, a governor must appear before the king. Now, you are very honest, and the king will find no fault in your governance of the country. However, when the king converses, he frequently moves from topic to topic and discusses sciences and languages. It would be proper and polite for you to be able to answer him, and so perhaps I should teach you sciences and languages."

This pleased the simple man. "I don't mind learning sciences and languages," he said to himself. He studied and mastered the sciences. Then he recalled what his friend the clever man had said to him, that it would be impossible for him ever to attain the other's intellectual capacity. "Now," the simple man thought, "I have attained his wisdom." Although he had become versed in sciences and arts, he did not let this interfere with his affairs, which he conducted straightforwardly as before.

Soon the simple man had his audience with the king. At first the two spoke about the governance of the province. The king was very pleased with the simple governor, for he saw that he acted justly and truthfully, without any corruption or dishonesty. Then the king began to discuss sciences. The simple man answered appropriately, and this pleased the king all the more.

"I see that he is a wise man," thought the king, "and yet he behaves with complete simplicity."

The simple man won great favor in the eyes of the king, and the king appointed him chief minister. He gave him an official letter of appointment to his post, and he ordered that an estate be given to him as his residence and that a beautiful palace, befitting his new status, be built there for him. All this was done: the palace was built on the estate that the king had given him, and the simple man assumed his great role with power and authority.

Now when the letter from the king had been delivered to the clever man, he said to the clever messenger, "Wait. Stay here overnight. We shall discuss the matter and come to a decision."

That night the clever man made a grand dinner for the messenger, and over the meal he began to analyze the situation, using all his learning and philosophy. "What can it mean," he exclaimed, "that such a great king sends for a lowly person like me? Who am I that the king should send for me? What can it mean? He is a great king, who rules a vast dominion and wields much power, and I am as nothing compared with him. Does it stand to reason that such a king would send for me? One could say that he summoned me on account of my wisdom, but what am I to the king? Has the king no wise men about him? The king himself must surely be a great sage! Why, then, should the king send for me?"

The matter confounded the clever man. As he wondered about it, he declared to the clever messenger, "Do you know what I think? There is no king, and everyone in the whole world is mistaken in believing that there is. Listen, does it stand to reason that the whole world should submit itself to one person and make him king over everything? No, it is clear that there is no king."

"But I brought you a letter from the king!" protested the messenger.

"Did you receive it from him personally?" the clever man asked him.

"No, someone else gave it to me."

"There! You can see for yourself that I am right. There is no king. Now tell me. You are from the royal capital, and you grew up there. Have you ever seen the king?"

"No."

"Now you can see that I am right. There is no king, for even you have never seen him."

"If that is so," returned the clever messenger, "who governs the country?"

"Ah, I can easily explain that. I am an expert in such matters, so you've asked the right person. I've traveled a great deal, and I spent some time in Italy, where I was able to learn the local customs. The country is ruled by seventy counselors, who remain in office for a limited period of time. All the citizens of the country take turns holding office, one after another."

His arguments began to influence the clever messenger, and finally the two agreed that there was no king.

"Wait," said the clever man. "Tomorrow I'll demonstrate even more convincingly that there is no king."

In the morning the clever man rose early and woke the clever messenger. "Come outside with me. I'll prove to you that the whole world is in error, and there is no king," he told his companion.

They went to the marketplace, and there they saw a soldier and stopped him short.

"Whom do you serve?" they asked him.

"The king," he replied.

"Have you ever seen the king?"

"No."

"You see!" exclaimed the clever man. "Could there be folly greater than this?"

Next they approached an officer, and they talked with him

until they found an appropriate opportunity to inquire, "Whom do you serve?"

"The king."

"Have you ever seen the king?"

"No."

"So!" cried the clever man. "Now you can see with your eyes that they are all mistaken and there is no king!"

The two were now in full agreement that the king did not exist. "Come, let us travel around the world!" exclaimed the clever man to his new friend. "I'll show you more examples of how everyone in the world is deluded by folly."

They departed together and traveled around the world, and everywhere they went they found the world to be in error. For them the matter of the king exemplified all delusions. Whenever they found people to be in error, they would tell each other, "That's as true as the story about the king!"

They continued traveling around the world, and eventually they used up all their money. They sold first one of their horses, then the other, and then the rest of their salable possessions, and had to wander around on foot. Still they were bent on investigating the world, and they continually found confirmation that the world was in error. They became footloose beggars and lost all their dignity and distinction. No one takes any notice of such beggars.

Eventually they came to the city in which the minister, the simple friend of the clever man, resided. In that city there lived a true Baal Shem, a Master of the Holy Name. This Baal Shem was highly regarded in the city, for he performed truly wondrous deeds, and he was renowned and held in great esteem even among the lords and nobles of the land.

The two clever men entered the city. As they walked around, they came upon the home of the Baal Shem and saw forty or fifty carriages with sick people waiting outside. The clever man thought that this must be the residence of a physician. As he was a great physician himself, he wanted to go in and make the other's acquaintance.

"Who lives in there?" he inquired of the people.

"A Baal Shem," they replied.

The clever man burst out laughing. "This is another lie, a further folly," he said to his companion. "This is even sillier than the fable about the king! Brother, let me explain this deception to you. The whole world is in the grip of error and lies like this one."

Meanwhile, they had grown hungry. As they had only three or four pennies left, they went to a cheap kitchen where one could get something to eat for such a tiny sum. "Give us something to eat!" they demanded, and they were served. While they ate, they talked and joked about the delusion and folly of believing in the Baal Shem.

The owner of the kitchen heard their banter and became very annoyed, for the Baal Shem was highly esteemed in that city. "Finish what's on your plates," he said, "and get out of here."

Then the Baal Shem's son came into the kitchen, but even then the two did not stop making jokes about the Baal Shem. The owner of the kitchen upbraided them for mocking the Baal Shem in the presence of his son, and finally he thrashed them and threw them out.

The two were most insulted, and they decided to bring a suit against the man. They consulted the owner of the hostel where they had left their packs about how to go about bringing such a suit. They explained that they had been assaulted by the owner of the kitchen. He asked them why the man had done such a thing, and they told him that they had been discussing the Baal Shem. "It is surely not right to beat people," replied the innkeeper, "but you had no right to talk about the Baal Shem as you did, for he is held in very high esteem around here." They saw that he too was in error, so they left him.

Next they approached a government official, a gentile. They

told him the story of how they had been beaten up, and he too asked them why. When they told him that they had been speaking derisively about the Baal Shem, he too thrashed them soundly and threw them out. They then went to a higher official, and then to an even higher one, but no one would give them a hearing. In every case they were thrashed and thrown out. Finally they reached the chief minister, who was the simple man.

The minister was informed by the guards in front of his residence that someone wished to see him. He gave orders that the man be allowed to enter, and so the clever man came before him. The minister recognized his old friend immediately, but the clever man did not recognize him, because he had achieved such high rank.

The minister spoke to him at once. "You see," he said, "where my simplicity has brought me: to this eminence! And where has your wisdom brought you?"

"So you are my old friend, the simple man!" exclaimed the clever man. "But we can talk about that later. Just now, I'm seeking justice against someone who beat me up."

"Why did he hit you?" asked the minister.

"Because I was talking about the Baal Shem," he replied. "I said that he was a liar and that the whole thing is nothing more than a big swindle."

"So you still cling to your cleverness!" exclaimed the simple minister. "Listen, once you said that you could easily reach my level, but that I could never reach yours. Now look: I attained yours long ago, but you have not yet reached mine. Now I can see that it is indeed more difficult for you to attain my simplicity."

Nevertheless, since he had known the clever man for a long time and remembered his former greatness, the minister instructed his servants to bring him clothes and dress him properly, and he invited him to dine with him.

During the meal the two began to converse, and the clever man expounded his opinion that there was no king.

"What are you saying?" cried the simple minister. "I've seen the king myself!"

"How do you know he is the king?" answered the clever man with a laugh. "Do you know him, and his father and his grandfather who were also kings? How do you know that he really is the king? People told you that he was the king, but they deceived you."

It greatly angered the simple man to hear his friend deny the existence of the king.

Meanwhile, someone approached them and said, "The devil is looking for you."

The simple man was terrified. He ran to his wife and told her fearfully that the devil was looking for him. "Send for the Baal Shem," she advised him, and so he did. The Baal Shem came and gave the minister amulets and other ways of protecting himself and told him that he need no longer be afraid. The simple man accepted what the Baal Shem told him with great faith.

Afterward the simple man and the clever man sat down together again. "What frightened you so?" the clever man asked his friend.

"The devil was looking for us!" replied the simple man.

The clever man laughed at him. "Do you really believe that there is a devil?" he asked.

"If not, then who sent for us?"

"It must be my brother," answered the clever man. "He wants to see me, and he made up the whole story."

"If that's really so, how did he get past the guards?" asked the minister.

"He probably bribed them, and they are lying when they say they haven't seen him," his friend replied.

Meanwhile, someone again entered, bearing the same message as before, "The devil is looking for you."

This time the simple man was not at all frightened, because

the Baal Shem had given him protection. "What have you got to say now?" he exclaimed to the clever man.

"I'll tell you what's going on. My brother is angry with me, and he's trying to frighten me with this trick."

He stood up and asked the person who had come with the message, "This fellow who has sent for us, what does he look like? What color hair does he have?" He asked a few more such questions, and the messenger answered accordingly.

"You see!" exclaimed the clever man. "My brother looks just like that!"

"Will you go with him?" asked the simple man.

"Yes, I'll go with him, but give me an escort of a few soldiers so that I won't be harassed."

The minister gave him an escort, and the clever man and his clever friend went off with the person who had come with the message. The soldiers soon returned alone. "Where are the two clever men?" inquired the minister. The soldiers replied that they had no idea. The two clever men had disappeared.

Actually the messenger had carried off the clever companions and thrown them into a swamp filled with dirt and lime, and there in the middle of it sat the devil on a throne. The mud was as thick as glue. The clever pair were stuck fast in it, unable to move. "Villains!" they cried. "Why are you tormenting us? There's no such thing as the devil. You're just scoundrels, and you've no reason to torment us like this!"

So the two of them wallowed in the swamp, and still they continued to inquire, "What is all this? They're just a bunch of hooligans. We must have quarreled with them on the road, and now they're getting their own back."

They remained in the swamp for several years, suffering horrible torments and afflictions. One day as the simple minister was passing by the home of the Baal Shem, he recalled his friend, the clever man. He went in to see the Baal Shem, bowed to him respectfully, and asked him, "Do you remember the clever man who was summoned and carried off by the devil and hasn't been seen since?"

"Yes, I remember," answered the Baal Shem.

"Could you possibly show me where he is and get him back?" the simple minister besought him.

"I can certainly show you the place," the Baal Shem replied, "and I can get him out, but no one else must go there, only you and I."

The two departed together. The Baal Shem did what he had to do, and they arrived at the place. The simple man saw the clever companions wallowing in the thick, muddy swamp. When the clever man saw the simple minister, he shouted, "Brother, look! They're beating me! These scoundrels are tormenting me cruelly, and for no reason!"

"Still you cling to your cleverness!" the minister exclaimed. "Do you still refuse to believe in anything? Do you still say that it is human beings who are doing this to you? Look, this is the Baal Shem whom you belittled, and he is the only one who can get you out of this."

The simple minister besought the Baal Shem to extricate the two and to prove to them that their tormentor was the devil and not humans. The Baal Shem did what he did, and the two found themselves standing on dry land. The swamp had disappeared, and the evil spirits had turned to dust. Only then did the clever man see the truth. He was forced to acknowledge that there really is a king and there really is a true Baal Shem.

Commentary

"The Clever Man and the Simple Man" is unique among Nachman's major tales in that the basic idea is explicit from beginning to end and is never veiled by allegory and symbolism. Nevertheless, allegory and symbolism are present and are essential to the story; the reader must understand the way they are employed in order to perceive both the deeper significance of the theme and the references to historical personalities and events.

Simplicity, or naïveté, occupies an important place in Nachman's teachings. This story treats the theme in a literary, non-hortatory manner; but in his other works, and especially in his oral teachings, Nachman demanded in an extreme, uncompromising fashion that his pupils abandon "cleverness" or "science," and that they devote themselves to simple and naïve faith.

Nachman perceives two polar approaches to life—the clever and the simple. The story depicts both paths and analyzes not only their significance but also the pitfalls and problems that are implicit in each. Despite the difficulties, Nachman's choice is clear—simplicity.

The single Hebrew word *hokhmah* (from the same root as *hakham,* the clever man of the story) encompasses many meanings: cleverness, the ability to understand, knowledge in a variety of fields (including science), and a spiritual mode of thought. Nachman seems to be willing to forgo them all in order to avoid the dangers implicit in some.

Nevertheless, the contrast at the center of the story lies not between knowledge and ignorance but between two spiritual characteristics: the ability and the inclination to probe, to seek for deeper meanings, and simplicity, seeing and accepting things as they are. Nachman perceives cleverness as intellectual disquiet, which is ultimately destructive. It leads inevitably to the abyss of doubt, it deprives the individual of the ability to live and to be content, and ultimately it ends in heresy.

Nachman is acutely aware of the dangers and the sacrifices involved in the path of simplicity, with its discarding of doubt and of deeper understanding. Nevertheless, he maintains that it is better that a man believe in everything, including truth, than that he deny everything, including truth. Moreover, this must be a conscious decision. Though it is possible that when a man reaches a high degree of simplicity, he may proceed farther into the realms of the intellect (as the simple man in this story is eventually able to do), there is no possibility of compromise about the basic approach and the early stages of spiritual development.

Nachman's formal ideological position is extreme, but in this literary elaboration he is somewhat more equivocal. There is never any doubt that the simple man is the hero and the exemplar of the tale, but he is depicted as a rather flat, stereoptypical figure. The clever man, on the other hand, is treated with greater depth and understanding. Nachman was personally acquainted with the agonies of cleverness; and even though his depiction of the clever man's progress is marked by uncompromising hostility and an irony that is frequently sharp, he was able to describe this character in convincing detail.

By skillful use of symbolism and allusion, Nachman extends the scope of the story far beyond an educational contrast between two types of people, two ways of life, and develops a powerful polemic against certain trends in Jewish thought. He was probably the only figure in his generation who dared to condemn all Jewish rationalist philosophy, and not just its more problematic aspects; rather than taking issue with particular theses or conclusions, as did several of his contemporaries, he attacked this philosophy in toto. The clever man in the story starts as a kind of Jewish rationalist philosopher and ends as an atheist. Nachman regards this path as an inevitable consequence, either explicit or implicit, of all such approaches to Judaism.

The two householders at the beginning of the story personify the established modes of Jewish life: they are rich—not only in the material sense—and the heritage they pass on consists of the large houses of age-old wisdom and tradition. Into such houses from time to time are born children with different personalities, each of whom interacts in his own way with his home and tradition. The major characters of this story are two such sons who differ deeply in their spiritual makeup: the one clever, quick-witted, and intelligent; the other simple and naïve.

It is clear that the simple man is no fool. The distinction between simplicity and folly is important in hasidic thought. Simplicity—even in the extreme manifestation of this story—is characterized by an awareness of itself and of its limitations. Folly, on the other hand, attempts to reconstruct reality according to one's limitations and feelings. It is thus not a natural deficiency but rather a failing that approaches sin. On a deeper level, this means that the simple man is closer to a true perception of reality. He may perceive things naïvely, and his understanding and grasp may be superficial, but his vision is not marred or distorted by untruthful ways of conceiving the world. The fool, on the other hand, always distorts the facts, wrenches them from their context, and thereby destroys their validity in order to make them accord with his own perceptions. To a certain degree, the more he learns, the greater is his power to despoil.

THE GREAT HOUSEHOLDS

The two great households (which, as I have previously noted, represent Jewish tradition) begin to fall into a decline. The tragedy of the weakening of traditional Judaism, symbolically represented by the impoverishment or the death of fathers, is a feature in several of Nachman's tales. Such declines are not specific to any historical period and, in fact, can take place at any time. When there are few great spiritual leaders and teachers in a generation, the rich heritage becomes an empty shell that cannot sustain the soul. In such circumstances the sons must fend for themselves.

THE PATH OF THE CLEVER SON

The simple son remains very close to his old home and takes up a humble vocation. For him, the sole consequence of the decline of his father's house is a lowering in his social and economic status.

The clever son, on the other hand, responds to his changed circumstances by seeking his fortune elsewhere. In many ways he is a typical "self-made" man. The first stage of his development is the feeling that he must break out of his immediate, stifling environment and discover the possibilities for growth that exist elsewhere. He goes out into the wide world.

It is important to understand the basic motivation of the clever son at this stage. He is not rebelling against his father or leaving an intolerable situation at home. On the contrary, he is doing no more than he was told to do. There is no symbolic abandoning of a heritage but a world tour that will be concluded by a triumphant homecoming. The problems begin only on the road itself.

The Clever Man and the Simple Man

Like so many ambitious men, the clever son accepts the first job offered him and exploits the first opportunity to move to a big city. It is here, in Warsaw, that we get the first inkling of one of the basic traits of his personality—restlessness combined with insatiable curiosity. Even at this early stage he is driven by the desire to acquire information and knowledge and to reach his conclusions "philosophically." He is thus not satisfied with his job, despite its rewards, and goes on to seek something even better. The choice of work as a shop assistant—or, specifically, the "rational reasons" for the choice—provide Nachman with the opportunity to begin to mock the clever man. Despite all his wisdom, he is attracted to the most superficial characteristics of status, the smart apparel of a servant. Such barbs become sharper and more frequent as the story progresses.

The clever son devotes all his energy to satisfying his curiosity and accumulating information. His restlessness takes him to distant lands. The wisdom he acquires is characteristic of his relativistic, pragmatic philosophy. Eventually it will make him world-weary.

Meanwhile, however, in his search for some kind of purpose, he acquires many skills. First he becomes a goldsmith—an occupation that requires intelligence and dexterity—then he becomes a jeweler, and then a physician. He is thus to all outward appearances a great sage, but the speed with which he learns indicates that these studies are not really meaningful to him. Ultimately his endeavors lack seriousness.

On the allegorical level, this episode refers to the acquisition of religious knowledge and represents a fierce attack on a certain species of Jewish scholar. There are Jewish sages who strive to master the realm of faith by means of rational inquiry and by gathering information. Though they retain a limited contact with the sources and with the ultimate purpose, on the inner, spiritual level this bond is gradually weakened and eventually lost. The erudition in Bible and Talmud that such a scholar may acquire is likened to a superficial skill without deep spiritual meaning, even though, like the physician, certain rabbis mend and repair the bodies and souls of others.

The first of the clever man's crises, the beginning of his decline and fall, is an outcome of his pride. At this stage he is not arrogant; nothing more than his justifiable pride in his own intellectual superiority leads him to pay the first penalty of cleverness. The very knowledge he possesses, his sureness of his own wit, and the intellectual superiority with which he examines the world, isolate him from his fellow men. His isolation forces him into a separate, incomplete world unto himself, and he can find no solace in the company of mortals. His decision to return home is both a result of his inability to find a place in the world and a relic of his old personality; but as long as he persists in his new ways, he will find no respite from torment.

THE SIMPLE SON

The simple son is not spared barbs of irony and sarcasm. Simplicity here is taken to an extreme, and the man's ignorance is abysmal. Even though he chooses a trade, shoemaking, that demands little understanding, and he works at it for a long time, his progress is scant. He remains an unskilled cobbler who must work long hours to earn a meager living. Nevertheless, though he must spend his days and nights in toil without even taking breaks to eat and has to endure what appears to be bitter hardship, he is always happy.

When we examine the description of the simple man on an allegorical level, we see a man at a relatively low spiritual level. What others achieve with facility, he has to struggle for and will possibly never reach. He represents a simple *zaddik*, a pious or saintly person who was common in early hasidic literature (the term, as in "The Master of Prayer," was also used as the title of a hasidic leader).

The Clever Man and the Simple Man

Of several other personalities who can be identified with the character of the simple man, the most prominent is Enoch, who in the Bible "walked with God, and was not, for God took him." According to the Midrash, Enoch began as a simple shoemaker who used to praise God with every stitch he made and eventually attained the exalted rank of Angel of the Divine Countenance. The simple man, too, is rewarded for his pure devotion, for God desires the pure intention in a man's heart even more than the quality of his deeds.

The simple man possesses an inexhaustible capacity for joy, which hasidic thought always considered to be a positive character trait. Were it not for this joy, he would have found his lot unbearable and would doubtless have fallen into despair. As it is, he can enjoy his plain diet in a way that the rich (and especially the clever man) cannot. He does not need dainty foods, for he finds all the delights of the world in whatever passes his lips. Implicit here is the notion that the sense of taste is subjective and depends on the person, not on the morsel. The Midrash says that the manna tasted different to every palate. Likewise, a single garment suffices for the simple man.

A further positive trait is presented: the simple man has no need to relate to the norms of society. When he completes a task, he is so pleased with what he has made that he is unaware of its defects. He is not critical, either of himself or of others, for criticism derives from the making of comparisons, from relativism—the viewing of everything according to extrinsic criteria —while the simple man's approach is intrinsic, and he is filled by what he has at any given moment. Once the shoe on which he has been working is finished and ready for use, he is overwhelmed with the joy of creativity. According to Nachman's teachings, the same applies to worship (indeed, a single Hebrew word means both work and worship): no matter how imperfect the prayers of the simple person, they are nevertheless something of rare excellence in his own eyes, and he has no cause to criticize them or seek out their defects.

The simple man's wife attempts to introduce a note of criticism, of comparison with others, but he totally rejects such evaluation: "What does that matter to me? What is theirs is theirs, and what is mine is mine." Another point in his reply concerns the reward for good deeds; this must never be calculated, for the reward lies in the doing itself.

A personality like the simple man's is inevitably the object of derision; people mock his way of life, his simplicity, and his faith, seeing them as manifestations of lunacy. His refraining from using his critical powers also makes him easy prey for practical jokers, against whom he defends himself with the rather inadequate request that they desist. Nevertheless, he does not emerge from these encounters as the underdog.

THE REUNION

The clever man returns home from his restless search for peace but finds his father's household in ruins. During his long peregrinations neglect has taken its toll; his doubting philosophy has destroyed his heritage or, at least, has made it empty for him. Furthermore, he has lost the ability to relate to the place and to its people. His home town has become an unsatisfactory inn. When eventually he accepts the offer of hospitality made by the simple man, he does receive something of the ancestral heritage, though only indirectly, through the medium of the respect and admiration of his old friend, who is in firm contact with it.

The clever man is unable to escape from torment, and whatever he does causes him suffering. If his work is perfect, no one else possesses the discrimination to appreciate it; if it is faulty, he is praised by those who cannot see flaws that are obvious to him. He is pathetically dependent on public opinion, and yet he disqualifies the opinions of others. He is isolated in the incommunicable pain of his own excellence.

The Clever Man and the Simple Man

According to Hasidism, depression and sadness are manifestations of arrogance and derive from comparing oneself with others. The simple man cannot understand such distress, while the clever man is so involved in himself that he is incapable of perceiving the source of the simple man's happiness or virtue. At this point the simple man decides that his own path is the better.

THE KING'S MESSAGE

Up to this point the story has revolved on certain material, psychological, or even historical axes. The king's message inviting the two men into his presence introduces a deeper theme: the consequences of their two paths for faith, and the relationship of man to God. The king in this story, too, clearly represents God. It should be noted that the two men are not ordered to come and are free to decide whether they will accept the invitation. The king's message is for the benefit of those to whom it is sent, not for that of him who sends it. Symbolically the king's message is Scripture, which is sent by means of different messengers, or interpreters, according to the understanding of its recipients.

The two messengers are sent not by the king himself (a direct command from God would terrify its recipients) but by an intermediary, the governor, the leading personality of his generation, who has been entrusted by the king with the governance of part of his realm. The simple man is also provided with new garments. This is of great symbolic significance, for in hasidic terminology garments are the external manifestations of the soul. Previously the simple man's soul had expressed itself in a rather coarse manner which had, however, been quite adequate to his circumstances. Now that he has been called to the king, he needs more refined garments.

Beggars and Prayers

The Simple Man's Way to the King

The simple man is not even able to read the king's letter and asks that the gist of the contents be explained to him. The simple messenger's reply—that the king wants him to come—is the ultimate, irreducible essence of the Bible. After the simple man has assured himself that this is no jest, he is filled with great joy. He has no clear concept of what the king is, but he does know that he is his lord and master. The simple man sets out without seeking to understand, leaving his wife's question unanswered.

The old governor is dismissed because he has become too clever. He no longer fulfills the king's desires as a simple agent and has begun to superimpose on his task his own human interpretations and considerations. The simple man is made governor for, though he is limited in intellectual ability, there is no doubt that he will rule faithfully. He has become a *zaddik* in the second sense: that of leader of a community. There are numerous such hasidic accounts of attainment of spiritual leadership by means of simplicity, devotion, prayer, and union with God. The simple man works with simplicity, which is now clearly presented not as the absence of critical faculties but as a positive virtue in its own right. He perceives things as they are, and all his actions are for the sake of justice and flow from justice.

The simple man is now able to grow intellectually, without impairing his essential fairness and without losing his simplicity. Because of his simplicity and his insight, he acquires wisdom without anguish, and by the time he reaches the king's presence, he has achieved such a high level that he is made chief minister. He now shows himself capable of ruling men and of placing his wisdom in the service of the king—both essential attributes of a *zaddik*.

The Clever Man and the Simple Man

The clever man responds to the king's message in a completely different way. First of all, he is in no hurry; even though the call is from the king himself, he prefers to wait—to sleep on it and think about it—before deciding whether he will comply. Subsequently his sophistry leads him to doubt everything. This part of the story is a brilliant parody of much medieval (and modern) rational philosophy. The validity of the letter (the Torah) itself is questioned. Can the king really need me? Or, if God is all wise and all powerful, why does He need me? Since the clever man does not understand the letter, something must be wrong. However, as one cannot say that God is mistaken, one must conclude that there is no God. This he substantiates with the invisibility of God, and he proceeds to doubt the reliability of all intermediaries. Many proofs for the existence of God are derived from the obvious order that exists in the world; and these, too, he disqualifies in the same facile way.

The clever man finally has a purpose in life, which he pursues with great zeal—to demonstrate that everyone else is wrong. His motivation is less a search for truth than a means to boost his own vanity and self-importance. If all other men are in error, then he is greater than they are. He starts his campaign with people who by virtue of their official function would appear to be in close proximity to the king, and discovers that none has seen him. On the allegorical level, this clearly relates to religious functionaries, most of whom accept the existence of God as a basic fact of faith; mystics who have direct experience of God are rare. Since the clever man and his companion judge everything only according to their own "rational" concepts, their beliefs are reinforced by every such discussion. They become further and further removed from the truth and from reality, and eventually their atheism becomes the basis of all their ideas and thoughts.

The two clever men gradually lose all their wealth, which is of course derived from the king, from the very God whose existence they deny. They lose all the respect that had previously been accorded them, for they go around seeking to prove to people something that would be pointless even if it were true, and that, being false, is utterly futile.

THE THIRD MEETING AND THE BAAL SHEM

The third meeting between the two old friends takes place as a result of the encounter of the clever man with a new personality, the wonderworker. Though this wonderworker is not modeled on a particular historical personality, he does reflect a reality well known to Nachman and his original readers. A wonderworker is not identical with a hasidic *zaddik*. The criterion for being a *zaddik* lies in the way he worships God.

In this episode Nachman is clearly taking issue with the many rationalist philosophers, Maimonides among them, who dismissed the belief in wonderworkers as mere superstition. However, this is more than a theoretical theological debate about whether the Baal Shem can perform miracles. Both the belief in the wonderworker and his actual miracles are objective elements within the plot, without which the ultimate salvation of the clever man cannot come about. When the clever man is traveling through the world trying to prove that there is no king, he is for the most part ignored, and he can persist unhindered in driving himself farther and farther from reality. When, however, he attempts publicly to discredit the Baal Shem, he draws on himself popular anger and even violence, which alter the direction of his career. He has reached a stage in his development from which he can no longer be saved by inner processes, external logic, or persuasion; only a miracle can save him. Furthermore, Nachman here highlights one of the greatest dangers of rationalism: when it is extreme, it becomes highly irrational. In rejecting personal experiences and observations that run counter to his rational ideas, the atheist is more irrational than any simple believer. In fact, he has become a counterbeliever who is as dogmatic and inflexible as those whom he seeks to illuminate. In his search for truth the clever man has abandoned intellectual honesty.

It is interesting to compare the two men in their new situations, in which their roles have been almost totally reversed. The simple man has become wise and speaks to his old friend from a position that is both critical and, up to a point, compassionate. His mind has developed, and he is able to deal with the most complex and subtle concepts and also has complete command of day-to-day matters. The clever man, on the other hand, has become totally involved in himself, almost to the point of lunacy. He can perceive nothing beyond his obsession. Once a rich man and a scholar of repute who was accorded great respect, he has become a pauper and an outcast. On meeting his old friend, he fails to recognize him and, when told the latter's identity, is utterly indifferent to him as a human being with whom he himself was once close. Instead, in a kind of monomaniac frenzy, he turns on him, too, with militant atheism. Previously the clever man has based all his arguments on the fact that nobody has actually seen the king, and thus, that belief in his existence was based only on blind, irrational faith. In the simple man, however, the clever man encounters someone who really has seen the king, one of those rare mystics who has direct personal experience of God.

The clever man's final argument in the face of a fact that he finds ideologically unacceptable is both futile and dishonest. There is no possible answer to the question of how one knows that what one perceives is really what it appears to be. The simple man has no way of explaining that seeing the king is an experience that excludes the possibility of doubt, and loses his patience with the clever man. The latter is now so locked within the circle of his tautologies that he can be saved only from without, by a painful experience that will force him once again to look at the world, to distinguish between it and his own inner thoughts. It is the devil who brings this about.

THE DEVIL

The devil has appeared several times in these stories, in a number of different manifestations—the angel of death, Satan, the powers of evil. Common to all is the fact that the devil, too, is subject to the divine law that governs the universe, and serves as an instrument of God's will. One of the functions of the devil is to act as a warning. In such a case he may appear as an objective natural phenomenon, or he may be experienced as a purely subjective feeling of impending evil. The proper response to such a premonition should be one of reaction—urgent and determined steps to reinforce the powers of good, both within oneself and in the world outside.

The problem of evil has always been one of the major pitfalls of rationalist philosophy, both Jewish and gentile. Rationalists tend to be optimistic in their picture of the world and allow no room for evil as a force that is palpable and that man must fight with and strive to overcome. In their attempt to explain certain phenomena that ideally should not be present in the world, they employ a number of philosophical strategems. Some say that evil does not really exist and is merely a local absence of good, just as darkness is the absence of light; and others say that evil is a byproduct of material existence and lacks both meaning and importance.

The Clever Man and the Simple Man

The clever man naturally refuses to accept the devil as a supernatural force and attempts to explain his own torments as being caused by ruffians or scoundrels. At one point he even identifies the devil as his own brother—one of Nachman's sharpest satirical barbs. The clever man and his companion are in a most pathetic and ludicrous state. They are cast into a pit of mire that is clearly symbolic of their cleverness, now totally degraded and valueless, and are being punished for sins they refuse to acknowledge. Their lack of self-awareness is absolute. There is now only one resolution. The simple man and the Baal Shem must together enter the realm of evil and extricate the clever man and his companion by faith and by miracle. This is an extremely perilous mission, which can be accomplished only by the holiest and most saintly of men. By now the simple man has attained such a status and can be seen as a hasidic *zaddik*, one of whose functions was to seek out the most abject sinners and raise them from evil. The story ends at the point from which the clever man can set out on a long and difficult path of rehabilitation.

Nachman told this story at a time when the Jewish enlightenment was gaining strength in Europe. He regarded this movement as potentially highly destructive to traditional Jewish society, and the fight against it as a national task of the utmost importance. He described in this story one of the weapons he sought to employ in this campaign—the appeal to individual Jews to abandon secular studies and return to naïve faith. However, the most powerful weapon he envisaged was the personality of the hasidic *zaddik*, a man who drew others to him and guided them in both religious and secular matters. In hasidic thought in general, and in Nachman's doctrines in particular, this new religious leader enjoyed a status that has no parallel in Jewish history. Such *zaddikim*, their unique personalities and their spiritual roles, are treated in detail and depth in "The Seven Beggars" and "The Master of Prayer."

[*147*]

The Seven Beggars

ONCE there was a king. This king had an only son, to whom he wished to transfer the kingdom during his own lifetime. On the appointed day, he held a great feast. When a king makes a feast, there is always great rejoicing, and all the more so on such a great occasion. Every one of the royal ministers, the dukes, and the nobles was there, and the common folk too shared in the day's gladness, because it is a great deed when a king abdicates in favor of his son. Everything was prepared to make the feast a truly joyous event, and musicians and jesters were there to entertain the guests.

At the height of the festivities, the king said to his son, "I am an astrologist, and I can foresee that a time will come when you will step down from the throne. When this happens, take care not to be sad. Be joyful. When you are joyful, I too shall be happy. I would be happy even were you to be sad, for it would show that you were unworthy of being king, and I would be pleased that you no longer ruled the land. But if you are joyful, I shall be very happy indeed."

The son took over the kingdom with great authority. He appointed royal ministers and had dukes, nobles, and an army at his command.

The new king was a very wise man. He was devoted to all forms of knowledge and maintained great sages at his court. Anyone who came to him bearing some new knowledge was accorded great respect, and the king would grant him wealth or honor, whichever was requested. Everything was given for wisdom.

Since wisdom was so important to the king, it soon became the pursuit of the whole kingdom. There was no one who was not engaged in some field of learning, some for the sake of money and others for the honor.

They devoted so much of their time to inquiring into the sciences that eventually they forgot the tactics of war. Even the most insignificant citizens were so learned that they would have been considered great sages in any other land, while the sages were wise beyond compare. As a result of their cleverness, these sages strayed into heresy, and they drew the king's son with them into heresy. But the simple people in the country were not harmed by the wisdom of the great sages and did not become heretics. This wisdom was very deep and subtle, and so the simple people could not understand it and were not harmed. Only the sages and the king became heretics.

There was good in the king's son; he had been born with virtuous qualities. Occasionally he would remember and reflect, "What have I come to? What am I doing?" He would sigh and deplore his sad state: "How could I have strayed into such things? What is happening to me? What will become of me?"

But every time this happened, he would soon begin to use his intellect, and his heretical ideas regained their sway.

One day the entire population of the country took flight. On the way they passed through a forest and lost there two small children of different families, a boy and a girl of about four or five. The children had nothing to eat, and they began to cry for food. As they wept, a beggar came by, carrying bags of bread. The children ran after him and clung to him. He gave them some bread to eat and asked them, "Where are you from, and how did you get here?"

"We don't know," they replied, for they were very small children.

The beggar turned to go, and the children pleaded with him to take them with him.

"I do not want you to come with me," he said.

Then the children noticed that he was blind. They were astonished by this, for they were unusually clever children, and they marveled that he was able to find his way without being able to see.

Before the blind beggar left, he blessed them with the words: "May you be as I am. May you be as old as I am." He gave them some more bread, and he went on his way.

The children realized that God was caring for them and that He had sent the blind beggar to feed them. But the bread that the beggar had given them did not last long, and again they cried for food. Night fell, and the children slept where they were in the forest. In the morning they still had nothing to eat, and they cried in hunger. Soon another beggar came. This beggar was deaf, and when they spoke to him, he made signs and said, "I hear nothing." He too gave them bread and turned to go. The children pleaded with him to take them with him, but he would not. And he too blessed them with the words:

"May you be as I am." Then he left some more bread and went on his way.

This bread too was soon finished, and the children once more began to cry. Yet another beggar came. They began talking with him, but his stuttering made his speech incomprehensible. He understood them well, but they could not grasp a word he said. He too gave them bread and, before he left, blessed them with the words: "May you be as I am." Then he went on his way.

The next day they were fed by a beggar with a crooked neck, and he too blessed them as had the others. A hunchbacked beggar came on the fifth day, then a beggar who had no hands, and finally a beggar who had no feet. Each gave them bread, and each one blessed them with the words: "May you be as I am."

When all the bread was finished, the children went in search of a place where people lived. Eventually they found a road which led them to a village. They entered one of the houses, and the people there took pity on them and gave them bread. At the next house, too, they were given food. Thus they became beggars. Things went well with them, and they vowed to stay together always. They made themselves big bags for the bread that people gave them, and went to all the celebrations, circumcisions, and weddings that were held in the area. Leaving the village, they went to beg in the larger towns. When there was a fair, they sat among the other beggars by the gates, holding out their plates for alms. Soon they became well known among the beggars, all of whom knew that they were the children who had been lost in the forest.

Once a great fair was held not far from a large city. All the beggars went there—the children, too. It struck the beggars that the two children would make a fine couple. The proposal quickly caught everyone's fancy, and the match was made. But how could a proper wedding for them be arranged? The beggars knew that on a certain day the king was to hold his birthday celebration. They decided that they would all go there and beg for meat and white bread for the wedding feast. And so it was. They begged whatever delicacies they could at the banquet, and afterward they gathered up the leftovers. Then they dug a pit so large that it could hold a hundred people, and covered it over with straw, dirt, and refuse. When it was finished, everyone assembled inside for the wedding.

The marriage ceremony was performed amid great rejoicing. The bride and groom, too, were very happy, but in the midst of their gladness they recalled the grace and kindness that God had shown them in the forest, and they wept with yearning. "If only the blind beggar who first gave us bread in the forest were here," they sighed. Immediately they heard the blind beggar call out, "Here I am!"

"I have come for your wedding," he told them, "and my wedding gift is that you be as old as I am. When you were little children in the forest I blessed you thus, and now I have come to give it to you as a gift for your wedding.

"You think that I am blind. In fact, I am not blind at all, but to me the time of the whole world is not worth a moment's fleeting glance. I am very old and still very young; despite my great age, I have not even begun to live. Not only do I say this of myself, but it has been confirmed to me by the great eagle.

"I shall tell you a story. Once some people were traveling in a great fleet of ships upon the sea. A tempest arose and smashed the ships, but all the people were saved. They reached a tower and climbed up into it, and there they found food, drink, and clothing of all kinds, and everything else that they needed. All the pleasures and comforts of the world were available there. After they had settled down, they decided that each should tell an ancient tale, the story of the very first thing he remembered. There were young and old among them, and they honored the oldest by asking him to speak first.

" 'What shall I tell you?' exclaimed the old man. 'I remember when the apple was cut from the bough.'

"No one understood his words, but the wise men among them said, 'Ah, that is indeed an ancient tale.' Then they honored the next oldest man and asked him to tell his story.

" 'That ancient tale,' he said, 'I too remember. But I also remember when the candle was burning.'

" 'That tale is even older!' exclaimed the sages, and they marveled that it had been told by the younger man.

"An elderly but still younger man was next to speak. 'I remember when the fruit began to take shape!'

" 'This story is older still!' said the sages.

"The fourth old man, who was younger than the other three, said, 'I remember when the seed was brought to be planted.'

" 'I remember the wise ones who conceived the seed,' said the fifth.

"The sixth one said, 'I remember the taste before it entered the fruit.' "

The blind beggar continued, "I was there on the tower, too. I was still a child then. 'I remember all those tales,' I said, 'and I also remember nothing.'

" 'That is indeed an ancient tale, older than all the rest!' exclaimed the sages, and they marveled that a child remembered more than any of them.

"After they had all told their tales, a great eagle alighted and knocked on the tower. 'Be paupers no longer!' he called. 'Return to your treasures and make use of them!' He told us that we must all leave the tower in order of age, the oldest first, and he began bringing us out. He took me first, for I was really the oldest. Then he took the younger people, and last of all the very oldest man. Whosoever was younger there was older, and the oldest man was the youngest of all.

" 'I shall interpret your stories and explain the meaning of what each of you remembered,' declared the eagle. 'The apple being cut from the bough, that is the severing of the navel cord. The candle burning, that is lying in one's mother's womb, when a candle burns above the infant's head. The fruit beginning to take shape, that is the body coming into being, when the child is first formed. The seed being brought for planting, that is the drop of semen being drawn into the womb. The wise ones who conceived the seed, that is the drop when it is still in the mind. The taste is the fragrance in the spirit, and the appearance is the soul. As for the child who said he remembers nothing, he is older than all the others, and he remembers what was before life, spirit, and the soul. He remembers nothingness, and this is highest of all.

" 'Return to your ships,' concluded the great eagle. 'They are your broken bodies, and they will be rebuilt. Go back to them now.' Then he blessed the people.

"To me," continued the beggar, "the eagle said, 'Come with me. You are like me, for you are very old and very young; despite your great age, you have not yet begun to live. I too am very old and very young, and so we are alike.'

"So you see, the great eagle has confirmed that I am very old and very young. Today I make this my wedding gift to you, that you will be as old as I am."

So the wedding feast was held amid great rejoicing and delight. On the second of the seven days of the celebration, the bride and groom remembered the deaf beggar and how he had saved them in the forest by giving them bread. "If only he were here now to share our joy," they sighed, and they wept with yearning.

At that very moment, he appeared. "Here I am!" he said, and he embraced and kissed them. Then he declared, "My gift to you today is that you be like me, that you lead a good life, as I do. When you were little, I only blessed you with this wish, and now I grant it to you completely as a wedding gift.

"You think that I am deaf," continued the second beggar. "In fact, I am not, but to me the whole world is worth nothing, so why should I listen to its cries of want? All the sounds in the world are brought forth by want; everyone cries out for what he lacks. Want is the source of even the joys in this world, for men are happy when they obtain what once they lacked. I, however, live a good life and lack nothing, and so these wants are not for my ears. The people of the land of wealth have confirmed that I live a good life." (This good life was that he ate bread and drank water.)

"There is a land of great wealth, whose inhabitants possess vast treasures. Once these rich people gathered together and boasted about the good lives they led; each one described the comforts and pleasures of his life.

" 'I live a better life than any of you,' I told them, 'and I can prove it. If you lead such good lives, you ought to be able to help a certain country that I know. In this country there was a garden, in which grew fruits with all the tastes and fragrances in the world, and there were also all kinds of sights, and all shapes, colors, and textures. There was a gardener in charge of this lovely place, and under his care it provided a good life for the entire country. Then the gardener disappeared, and since there was no one to tend them, all the good things in the garden ceased to flourish. Even so, it was still possible to live off the wild fruits that continued to grow there. A cruel king attacked the country. He was unable to harm the people, and so he set out to spoil the good life they had derived from the garden. He did not do this by destroying the garden itself, but by means of three bands of slaves who did his bidding. The task of the first band was to spoil the sense of taste by making everything taste like rotting flesh. The task of the second band was to spoil the sense of smell by imparting to every fragrance the bitter odor of galbanum. The third band spoiled the appearance of all things by darkening the people's vision, as though heavy clouds covered their eyes.

" 'Now, if you really live a good life,' I told the rich people, 'help this country. But I warn you, if you do not help them, these same three misfortunes will be your lot, too.'

"The rich people set out for the country of the garden, and I went with them. On the way, they continued to live their customary good lives, for they were all very rich. As they came closer to the country, however, they felt that the taste and the smell and the appearance of everything were becoming spoiled. 'You haven't yet reached the country,' I told them, 'and already your senses are blighted. What will happen when you get there? Will you be able to help its people?'

"I gave them some of my own bread and water to eat and drink. In my plain fare they found every kind of taste, smell, and appearance, and their spoiled senses were made good.

"Meanwhile, the people of the country of the garden themselves began to seek a way to restore their corrupted senses. They had heard of the wealthy country, and they thought that the lost gardener must be of the same origin as the people who lived the good life. So they decided to send to that country for help. Messengers were dispatched, and on their way they encountered the very people they were seeking.

" 'Where are you bound?' the wealthy people asked the messengers.

" 'We are going to seek help from the country of wealth,' the latter replied.

" 'We are from the country of wealth ourselves,' exclaimed the travelers, 'and we are on our way to you.'

" 'But they need me,' I told the travelers, 'for you will not be able to save the country. Stay here, and I shall go with the messengers.'

"I accompanied the messengers back to their country and entered one of its cities. Some people drew near the place where I was standing. They were joking with one another, and soon more and more people gathered around, all of them joking and laughing. I listened to what they were saying and heard obscenities. One of them would say something lewd, another would say it more subtly, a third would laugh, and so on and so forth.

"I went on to another city, and there I saw two people arguing about a business deal. They went to court to settle the dispute, and the judges pronounced one of them innocent and the other guilty. As soon as they left the court, they began to quarrel again. They were not satisfied with the judgment and decided to take the matter to another court. After the matter was once more settled, one of them began arguing with someone else, and these two decided to go to yet another court. Thus all of the people were continually arguing and bringing their disputes to one court after another, and thus it was the whole city was full of courthouses. I investigated the situation and saw that it had come about because no one cared for truth. The judges all took bribes, so that if one judge decided in someone's favor, another might just as well decide against him, for their decisions were never based upon truth.

"Then I saw that the country was filled with promiscuity. The people had been so corrupted by fornication that they considered it quite permissible.

"I told the people that it was these things that had spoiled their senses, and I showed them how all had been wrought by the three bands of slaves assigned by the cruel king to undermine the country. One band had gone around speaking coarsely and so had introduced obscenity into the country. Obscenity had so corrupted the sense of taste that all things seemed to taste of carrion. Another band had introduced bribery into the country, and this had corrupted the sense of sight. The people's eyes were clouded, for, as it is written in Scripture, 'Bribery blinds the eyes of sages.' The third band had brought promiscuity into the land, and this had corrupted the sense of smell.

" 'Therefore,' I told them, 'you must rid your country of these three sins. Seek out the men who introduced these abominations and banish them. When you have thus purified the land, not only will your senses be restored, but you will also be able to find your lost gardener.'

"They did as I had told them. In order to seek out the slaves who had done the cruel king's bidding, they seized people and asked them, 'Where did you come from?' In this way all the slaves were isolated and banished, and the country was purified of the three sins.

"Meanwhile, people began to talk about a lunatic who walked the streets claiming that he was the gardener. Everyone had thought that he was mad, and people used to throw stones at him and drive him away. But perhaps he was really the gardener. He was brought to me, and I declared, 'This man is indeed the gardener.'

"When they saw how I had restored that country, the people of the land of wealth agreed that I live a good life. Now I grant you my good life as my wedding gift."

The happiness and rejoicing at the wedding celebration grew even greater, for both long life and a good life had been bestowed on the young couple in the presence of all.

On the third day of the feast, the bride and groom wept with yearning once more as they remembered their days in the forest. "If only the beggar who stuttered were here to share our joy," they sighed.

As they sat longing for him, he entered the place where they were celebrating, the great pit dug by the beggars. "Here I am," he cried, and he embraced and kissed them. Then he too began: "In the forest I blessed you with the wish that you should be as I am, and now I grant it to you as a wedding gift.

"You think that I am heavy of speech," he continued. "In fact, I am not really a stutterer at all. I am unwilling to speak, because all that man says that is not uttered in praise of God is wanting. In fact, I am extraordinarily eloquent; I am a master of poetry and speech. I can recite such marvelous parables, poems, and songs that when I begin to speak, there isn't a creature on earth that does not desire to listen, and in my words there is all wisdom. This has been confirmed to me by the great man who is called 'the man of true grace.'

"Once all the wise men were sitting together, and each one was boasting of his science. One of them claimed that he had invented the smelting of iron. Another said that he had invented the extraction of silver, which was more important. But then someone else said that he had discovered how to purify gold. Another wise man boasted that he had invented the instruments of war, and yet another claimed that he could extract metals from ores never used for this purpose. Others boasted of having made other important inventions by means of science, such as gunpowder and explosives.

"As they sat there boasting of their science, one of them said, 'I am wiser than all of you, for I am as wise as the day.' No one there understood what he meant.

" 'If all your sciences were added together,' he explained, 'the sum would amount to no more than a single hour. Each of the sciences is derived from one of the seven days of Creation, and all man's science is is to assemble various elements that were created on a particular day. All of your wisdom, if it could be summed up, would amount to no more than that of a single hour of Creation—but I am as wise as a whole day.'

" 'As which day?' I asked the wise man who had just spoken.

'This man is wiser than I am!' he exclaimed. 'He asks which day. But, in fact, I am as wise as any day you wish.'

"How, then, did my question show me to be the wiser? He, too, is as wise as any day he wishes. But that is a whole story in itself.

"The man of true grace is a very great man," continued the beggar. "I gather and bring to him all acts of true grace. And time itself is created by acts of true grace.

"At one end of the world there is a mountain. On the mountain is a rock, and from the rock flows a spring. At the other end of the world is the heart of the world. Everything has a heart, even the world itself. The heart of the world is the perfect form of man, with a face, hands, and feet, but even its toenails possess more heart than the actual heart of any other being.

"The spring and the heart face each other from the two ends of the world. The heart yearns greatly for the spring and wishes to come to it. Its desire is so great that it cries out with yearning. The spring, too, longs for the heart.

"This heart suffers in two ways. The first is the burning heat of the sun. The second is its terrible yearning for the spring, which it eternally faces from afar, longing for it with all its soul and crying out to reach it.

"When the heart has need of a little respite to revive its spirit, a great bird comes and shades it from the sun with its outspread wings. But even in these moments of rest, the heart gazes at the spring and never ceases to yearn for it.

"If the heart pines so deeply for the spring, why does it not go to it? The reason is that were it to move toward the mountain, the slope would vanish from its sight, and it would no longer be able to see the spring. Were that to happen, the heart would die, for its very life depends upon the spring. And were the heart of the world to perish, heaven forbid, the entire world would cease to exist, for just as the heart is the life of every being, so the world itself cannot continue to exist without its heart. Thus the heart can never come to the spring and stands forever facing it, yearning and crying for it from the depths of its soul.

"The spring has not time of its own, for it does not exist within time. How, then, can it continue to exist in the world? It receives time as a gift from the heart, day by day. When each day draws to a close, no time is left for the spring, and it is on the verge of disappearing. Were the spring to disappear, the heart, too, would die, heaven forbid, and the world would cease to exist. And so, as the day draws to a close, the heart and the spring bid each other farewell with wondrous parables, poems, and songs, with words full of love and yearning.

"The man of true grace watches over all this, and just before the end of the day, he presents the heart with the gift of another day, and the heart presents this day to the spring, and so the spring once again has time to exist. The new day, too, comes from wheresoever it was with wondrous parables and songs that are full of all wisdom. Just as one day differs from another, for there are different days of the week and new moons and festivals, so too do the parables and songs differ.

"But know, the time that the man of true grace presents to the heart he receives from me, for I gather the acts of true grace that make up time. I am wiser than the wise man who boasted that he was as wise as any day he wished, for all the days of time, with their wondrous parables and songs full of wisdom, are from me. The man of true grace has confirmed that I can speak in parables and songs of all wisdom. Now my gift for your wedding is that you shall be like me."

At the wedding feast, the rejoicing grew still greater.

That day's celebration ended, and they slept. In the morning, the two children remembered the beggar with the crooked neck, and they longed for him too to come and share in their wedding celebration.

Just as they were yearning to see him once more, he entered the pit. "Here I am!" he exclaimed, and he fell upon their necks and kissed them. Then he too told them of his gift. "In the forest," he began, "I blessed you with the wish that you would be like me. Now I give you this as my wedding present.

"You think that I have a crooked neck. In fact, my neck is straight and fine, but I twist it to prevent my breath from mingling with the foolish vanities of men which fill the world. My throat is beautifully formed, and I have an excellent voice, with which I can imitate every sound in the world that is not speech. This has been confirmed to me by the people of the land of music.

"In that land, everyone is versed in the art of music. All of the people spend their days making music, and there is no one, not even the smallest child, who does not play some musical instrument. The least of them would be considered a great artist in any other country, and their king and his orchestra are gifted with truly extraordinary talent.

"Once the greatest musicians of this country were sitting together, boasting of their abilities. One boasted that he could play this instrument, and one that he could play another instrument. A third declared that he could play both their instruments, and a fourth that he could play all the instruments in the world. Then one of them boasted that he could imitate a particular instrument with his voice. Another said that he could imitate the sound of some other instrument, and someone else that he could imitate the sound of any instrument. One triumphantly announced that he could imitate even the sound of a drum, but another bettered his claim by vaunting his ability to imitate a cannon shot.

"I was there as well. 'My voice is superior to any of yours, and I'll prove it to you!' I exclaimed to them. 'If you are such wonderful musicians, let us see whether you can save two suffering countries. These countries are a thousand miles apart. None of their people sleeps at night, for at dusk a great wail goes up over each land, so loud and so mournful that all who hear it begin to wail themselves. All the people, men, women, and children, spend their nights in a deep, clamorous lament that would melt a stone. If you are such great musicians, let's see if you can save these two countries, or even imitate that dreadful wailing sound.'

" 'Will you take us there?' they asked me.

" 'Yes, I shall,' I told them.

"They made all the necessary preparations, and I led them to one of the two unfortunate countries. Night fell, and, as always, the wailing began. Before long the musicians too began wailing, along with everyone else, and they quickly realized that they could do nothing to help this mournful land.

" 'Can you at least tell me the source of this terrible wail?' I asked them.

" 'Do you know it yourself?' they asked.

" 'Yes, I do,' I told them. 'There are two birds, a male and a female, and they are the only pair of their kind in the world. Once the female was separated from the male and lost her way. Her mate searched for her, and she too sought him everywhere. They both looked for each other for a very long time, but they only strayed farther and farther apart. When they realized that they could not find one another, they stayed where they were and built themselves nests. The male built his near one of the two countries—not right next to it, but near enough that its people could hear his voice—and the female built hers near the other. When night falls, the two begin to wail with yearning for one another. Their cries, loud and mournful, are heard throughout both lands, drawing forth the lament of all their inhabitants and driving away their sleep.'

"The musicians were reluctant to believe this tale. 'Can you take us to see these birds?' they asked me.

" 'Yes, I can take you to where they are,' I told them, 'but how can you undertake to approach them? Even from here you are unable to withstand their lament, and begin to wail yourselves. Were you to go there, you would find it unbearable. Nor can you approach the place by day, for at daybreak other birds flock to each of the pair, consoling them and making them laugh with joy. "You will still find each other," they tell the mournful pair, and the efforts of the birds to raise their spirits are so successful that the sound of their rejoicing is also impossible to bear. Although the call of their lament spreads far and wide, the sound of their merriment can be heard only nearby. And so you cannot go near the place, either by day or by night.'

" 'Can you reunite the two?' the musicians asked me.

" 'Yes, I can,' I told them, 'for not only can I imitate every sound in the world, but I can also throw my voice, so that it is heard far away but not where I am. I can imitate both their voices, and by sending hers to him and his to her, I can lead them closer and closer together until they are united.'

"But who would believe such claims? I led the musicians into a wood. They heard the sound of a door being opened and then closed and locked with a snap of the latch. A shot rang out, the hunter called to his dog to fetch the quarry, and they heard the dog rummaging and dragging something through the snow. But when they looked around, they saw nothing whatever, nor did they hear any sound issuing from any mouth. Then all the great musicians of the country agreed that I have a marvelous voice and can imitate any sound in the world. Now, for your wedding present, I grant you that you will be like me."

On the fifth day, amid the gaiety of the wedding feast, the bride and groom remembered the hunchbacked beggar and yearned to see him. "If only he were here," they said, "how happy we would be."

Sure enough, he soon stood before them, saying, "Here I am. I have come to your wedding." He embraced and kissed them, and then he too told them of himself and of his gift.

"When you were little children," he said, "I blessed you with the wish that you would be like me. Now I grant you this as my wedding gift to you.

"I am not a hunchback at all; in fact, my shoulders are so powerful as to be 'the little that holds the great,' and I shall tell you how this was confirmed to me.

"Once a group of people gathered to talk, and each boasted that he could be called the little that holds the great. One of them was ridiculed, the claims of the rest were accepted, but my ability was accepted as the greatest of all.

"The first of them claimed that his mind could be called the little that holds the great, for he bore tens of thousands of people, with their needs, actions, passions, and all the events of their lives, in his small brain.

"The others laughed at him. 'You are nothing, and all the people in your mind are nothing,' they declared.

" 'I once saw an example of the little that holds the great that resembles yours,' one of them said. 'I was passing by a mountain, and I saw a huge pile of refuse and filth on its slopes. There was so much of it that I wondered how it got there. "It all comes from me," said a man who was standing nearby. It turned out that he dwelt close by the mountain, and there he threw the leavings of his meals and all the rubbish and filth he produced. A vast heap of garbage came from this one man, and so, like you, he could be called the little that holds the great.'

"Another claimed that the attribute of the little that holds the great applied to his tiny country. Its fields and orchards produced such great amounts of fruit that when all the crops were gathered, they exceeded what could possibly have grown in such a small area. This, declared the man, was the little that holds the great, and the others all agreed.

"The next speaker said that he had a wonderful orchard. It was so beautiful that many people, including ministers and aristocrats, would come there for a summer's stroll, and more people actually entered it at any one time than the garden could possibly hold. This garden too, he said, could be called the little that holds the great, and his words were also well received.

"Another said that his speech could be described as the little that holds the great. 'I am secretary to a great king,' he explained. 'Many people present requests, petitions, and various other matters to the king, but he is of course unable to give his attention to each and every one of them. Instead, I combine all their petitions, praises, and requests and pass them on to the king in a few well-chosen words. Thus, my speech is the little that holds the great,' he concluded.

"The following speaker claimed the same quality for his silence. He had a great many adversaries, and they were continually quarreling with him in his presence and slandering him behind his back. All that they said he met with silence, and his silence responded to so many words of calumny that it too could be considered the little that holds the great.

"The last one said that he himself was the little that holds the great. There was a poor man, he related, who was blind and huge in stature. He was small himself, but he guided this poor, blind man. Were it not for him, the huge man would slip and fall, and so he considered himself 'the little that holds the great.'

"Now," continued the hunchbacked beggar, "I told them, 'You all possess something of the little that holds the great, and I know what each one of you meant by his words. I know, too, why the last to speak, who told us that he leads the huge blind man, is the greatest of you. It is he who leads the moon, which is called blind because it has no light of its own. He is small, and the moon is great—for the world could not exist without it —and so he can truly be considered the little that holds the great. But my claim to the quality is greater than any of yours, and I can prove it. Let me tell you a story.

" 'Once a group of people were making a study. Every animal, they knew, has a particular shady spot where it chooses to abide. Every bird too has a bough upon which it rests, and there it perches, nowhere else. The people wondered whether there was a single tree in whose shade every animal would want to lie and in whose branches every bird would find its place. They discovered that such a tree did exist, and that animals and birds of every kind lived there, all mingling and playing together and never harming each other. They desired very much to go to that tree, for they realized that the joy of being there must surely be boundless. They tried to ascertain in which direction they should go, but could not agree among themselves, and there was no one to decide who was right. One said they would go to the east, another to the west, and others were just as strongly in favor of the other two directions. Then a wise man came to them and said, "Why are you inquiring about the direction? First you should find out which of you can go there. Not everyone is worthy of going to the tree, only those who share its qualities. Faith in God, fear of God, and humility are its roots, and its trunk, from which its branches grow, is truth. Whosoever does not possess these attributes cannot approach the tree." Some of them did have such attributes, but others did not. As they were all of one group and did not want to be separated, they decided to wait until all were worthy, so that they could all go together. They worked to improve themselves, and when all were worthy, there were no longer any differences of opinion about the right direction. They set out together on their way to the tree. They traveled for a long time, until at last they saw the tree from afar. When they looked at it, however, they realized that the tree did not exist in space; it had no place. But if it did not exist in space, how could they reach it? I, too, was with them, and I told them I could lead them to the tree. The tree had no place, because it existed beyond space. Now, the little that holds the great—the small place that holds more than it possibly can—does occupy space, for no matter how small it is, it must occupy some space. I embody the highest form of the little that holds the great, for I stand at the very limit of space, beyond which there is no space. I could bring them to the tree which is beyond space, for I am the threshold between space and beyond space. I brought them to the tree, and that is how I received confirmation that I am the highest form of the little that holds the great.

"Now I give this to you, so that you will be like me." The joy of the wedding celebration continued, made even greater by the gifts the young couple had received.

As their rejoicing entered its sixth day, the newlywed couple yearned to see the beggar who had no hands. They had not been thinking of him long when he entered the pit and said, "Here I am! I have come to your wedding." He embraced and kissed them, and he too granted them the fulfillment of his blessing.

"You believe that my hands are stumps," the beggar told

them, "but they are really quite sound. In fact, they are extraordinarily powerful, but I do not use my strength in this world, because I need it for another purpose. This was confirmed to me at the castle of water.

"There was a king who desired a princess. He devised many plots to capture her, and finally he succeeded in bringing her to his side. One night the king dreamed that the princess rose and killed him. He awoke with a start, and his memory of the dream troubled him deeply. He called for all his soothsayers, and they said that the dream meant that she would indeed kill him.

"The king did not know what to do with her. He could put her to death, but this would upset him. He could also banish her, but the very thought angered him, for after all his efforts to obtain her, she would be taken by some other man. In any case, were he to let her go, the dream would surely be fulfilled, for once she was under the protection of another she could return and kill him. But he feared death at her hands were he to let her remain in his court. He could not decide what to do, and meanwhile, because of his fears, his love for her began to diminish. Gradually it disappeared, and she, too, gradually ceased loving him. Eventually she came to hate him, and she fled from the court. The king sent out his scouts to search for her, and when they returned they reported that she had taken refuge by the castle of water.

"The castle of water is surrounded by ten walls of water, one inside the other. Within the castle, the very ground one walks upon is water, and so are the garden and all the trees and fruit that grow therein. The beauty and splendor of this castle surely need no description, for a castle all of water is a great marvel. No one, of course, can enter it, for, since the whole castle is made of water, anyone who tried to enter would drown.

"The princess, in her flight, had reached the castle, and now she was circling around it. This, too, was reported to the king, who assembled his army and set out to capture her. When the princess saw them, she decided to run into the castle, for she preferred drowning to being caught by the king and forced to return with him. Then, too, there was always the chance that she would survive her leap into the waters and succeed in entering the castle.

"The king saw her running into the water. 'So that is how it is,' he said to himself, and he commanded his soldiers to shoot at her; if she perished, he thought, so be it. They shot, and she was struck by all the ten kinds of arrow with their ten kinds of poison. She continued her flight into the castle, and she passed through the gates of all ten watery walls (for there are gates in the walls of the castle of water) to reach the inner court. There she fell and remained in a deep faint.

"Once I told this story to some people, who had all been boasting about the strength of their hands. Each had described a great feat that testified to his power.

"One boasted that his hands were so powerful that he could catch and retrieve an arrow after he had shot it from his bow.

" 'What kind of arrow can you retrieve?' I asked him. 'There are ten kinds of arrow, and on the tip of each is smeared a different kind of poison. Each of the ten inflicts a different kind of harm, and each one is more powerful than the last. Which kind can you retrieve? And can you retrieve the arrow only before it strikes, or even after it has hit the mark?'

" 'I can retrieve the arrow even after it has struck its prey,' he answered.

" 'But what kind of arrow can you retrieve?' I asked again.

"He described the particular kind of arrow to which his strength applied. 'If you can retrieve only one kind of arrow,' I said, 'you cannot heal the princess.'

"Another boasted that his hands were so powerful that when he received, he was actually giving, and therefore he is always a great giver of charity.

" 'There are ten kinds of charity. Which kind do you give?' I asked him.

"He answered that he gave the tithe of one in ten. 'If you give only this charity,' I exclaimed, 'you cannot heal the princess, for you can penetrate only the first of the walls that surround her.'

"Another man boasted of his power to bestow the wisdom that all the leaders of the world needed just by laying his hands on their heads.

" 'There are ten kinds of wisdom. Which kind can you bestow?' I asked him.

"He described the particular kind of wisdom he could bestow. 'You cannot heal the princess,' I told him, 'for you cannot know her pulse. There are ten kinds of pulse, but if you can bestow only one kind of wisdom, you can know only one of them.'

"Yet another man boasted that his hands were so strong that he could hold back a tempest and make it into a pleasant breeze.

" 'There are ten kinds of wind. Which one can you hold back with your hands?' I asked him.

"He told me which of the winds he was able to conquer, and I said to him, 'You too cannot heal the princess, for you cannot play the melodies she needs to hear. She can be healed by ten kinds of melodies, but you can play only one of them.'

" 'And you, what can you do?' they asked me.

" 'I have all the powers that you have,' I answered, 'and I can do what you cannot. Each of you has only a tenth part of the power of which you boast, but I possess all the other nine parts as well.'

"Only I can heal the princess, for he who does not possess all ten kinds of charity in his hands cannot pass through the ten walls of water; he would drown in the attempt. The king and his soldiers pursued the princess and were drowned, but I can penetrate all ten walls of water.

"These walls of water are the waves of the sea that 'stood like a wall,' and they are raised up by the wind. The waves that form the walls stand there always, but it is the wind that supports them. I can pass through each of the ten walls of the castle of water, and I can remove all ten kinds of arrow from the body of the princess. With my ten fingers I can feel each of the ten kinds of pulse, and I can heal the princess by means of ten kinds of melody. Thus I can heal the princess completely, and that is the confirmation of the great power that I bear in my hands. Today I am giving you that power as my wedding gift."

The gladness of the wedding feast was greater than ever, and all who were there were very joyful indeed.

(Here the narrative ends. For the story of the seventh beggar and the end of the story of the king's son, Rabbi Nachman said he will never tell.)

Commentary

"The Seven Beggars" is Nachman's final tale, and he himself regarded it as the climax of his literary activity. Related a few months before his death, when he was already gravely ill, the story is without doubt a magnificent conclusion to his work and a masterpiece from the point of view of both content and literary style. To a certain degree it serves as a summary of and commentary on the earlier tales, from which it picks up and develops motifs. The central theme is similar to that of "The Master of Prayer"—the role of the *zaddik* in bringing about the Redemption—but here the emphasis is more on the *zaddik*'s theological, almost cosmic functions, and less on his work among men. The story is extremely rich in imagery and combines in an artistic unity biblical, talmudic, and kabbalistic sources together with a certain amount of worldly wisdom and elements of folk tales. The structure of the tale is also very fine, despite the fact that it was never finished—or, rather, that it has no conclusion—and is more complex than any of the others. The story as a whole is made up of an outer narrative framework (the king and his son) and an inner narrative framework (the children and the beggars) which provides the setting for six of the beggars' tales. Furthermore, the beggars' tales are all cast in the same literary form, with each beggar relating how he won a competition.

THE OUTER NARRATIVE FRAMEWORK—
THE KING AND HIS SON

The outer narrative framework is in fact no more than the beginning of a story that is never concluded. In rich symbolic language, it describes the condition of man in the Garden of Eden. The story breaks off after the sin but before the expulsion from Eden, and the thread is never resumed. Logically its ending would have been the restitution of the sin of Adam and the messianic Redemption.

As in most of the other tales, the old king clearly represents God. The abdication of the king during his lifetime is a metaphor for the way that God, having created man, gives him dominion over the world, and the great feast refers to the story of the celebration held by the Heavenly Host at the end of the Creation. The description of the king as an astrologer who knows that at some time in the future his son will be deposed, but not how the latter will react to this state of affairs, reflects the apparent contradiction between divine omniscience and the free will given to man.

One of the central characteristics of hasidic thought was the injunction against being sad. Unlike bitterness, which can be productive, sadness was regarded as a kind of self-indulgence that drains man of his spiritual resources. A person who is sad about having sinned, for example, loses the capacity for change and is likely to be caught in vicious circles from which there is no exit: sin creates feelings of guilt, which generate sadness and dejection, which lead to despair and to surrender to the urge to sin again. The hasidic prescription, which the king gives his son here, is to strive for a good disposition, to will oneself to be happy even in bad times. The sin that eventually seduces the king's son is the pursuit of wisdom as an end in itself, just as the sin of Adam was to eat the fruit of the tree of knowledge. In a continuation of the theme of "The Clever Man and the Simple Man," Nachman shows how such wisdom leads to heresy. The idea that excessive concentration on the intellectual side of life can make one forget the art of war is derived from a classical treatment of the fall of Jerusalem, but here it also refers symbolically to negligence in the day-to-day struggle with evil.

THE INNER NARRATIVE FRAMEWORK

There is no explicit causal relationship between the outer and the inner narrative frameworks, beyond the fact that one precedes the other chronologically. Though it has been suggested that the flight of the entire nation at the beginning of the inner narrative is the result of the king's son having forgotten the art of war, there is no textual basis for this. What is clear is that there has been a great catastrophe, and that the few survivors are those who can provide a fresh start for humanity. They are a new creation, a new generation that can set right what their predecessors have spoiled.

The two children who are lost in the forest are not described as possessing individual identities or personalities, and they remain a dual entity throughout the story. They can be seen as symbolizing either the Jewish people as a whole or as its best part. The beggars who save the children from starvation are the seven great spiritual providers of the Jewish people, who were active in their own times and also served as paradigms of parallel leaders in later generations. They are Abraham, Isaac, Jacob, Joseph, Moses, Aaron, and David (though they do not appear in the story in this order), who are collectively known in mystical sources as "the seven shepherds."

The word *beggar* is highly significant, for the Hebrew for it also means *seeker*. By devoting their lives to the quest for sparks of holiness that are immanent in the world yet exiled from it, the beggars are seeking a connection to divinity. The individual deformities that characterize each of the beggars will be explained in the discussion of each tale, but here I should note that they are in fact only apparent defects: they are like photographic negatives that render white as black. Qualities that are intrinsically perfect are perceived externally as faults. The children realize this intuitively when they ponder the fact that the blind beggar seems to know the way through the forest, and they immediately accept his guidance. Together the defects of all the beggars—or rather their opposites—make a complete human figure. This reflects a profound and esoteric kabbalistic doctrine which develops the biblical verse that man was created in God's image into the idea that there is a link between each external organ and each of the ten *Sefirot,* the divine manifestations. Man's task in the world is to bring himself to perfection —that is, to re-create himself according to the divine image and thereby to redeem himself and the world.

The fact that each beggar gives the children only a little bread and then leaves them to fend for themselves reflects a bitter historical reality. Great leaders are few and far between, and in the interim periods the people must subsist on the spiritual sustenance given them in earlier times.

The blessings that the beggars give the children refer, of course, to inner qualities and not to defects; but for the sake of the narrative this is not made clear until much later. The act of blessing someone, the paradigm of which is to be found in the biblical story of the patriarchs, is to pass on to another a gift that one has received oneself. It is a method by means of which spiritual existence transcends the barriers between people, and it is a manifestation of the donor's desire to remain in the world indefinitely by imparting his experience and essential humanity to those whom he considers worthy.

With each encounter the children develop spiritually; and eventually they, too, become beggars, seekers after the sparks of holiness. At this point they must marry for, according to Jewish sources, only when man and woman are united can they reach perfection.

The wedding celebration seems to combine two major Jewish festivals, the New Year (Rosh Hashana) and the Feast of Tabernacles (Sukkot). The day of the king's birthday celebrations, on which the beggars could ask for and obtain whatever they desired, is the New Year, "the remembrance of the first day," which is also a day of judgment when God decides what each person will receive in the coming year. The resemblance to the Feast of Tabernacles is even more striking. This is a seven-day festival, and the place the bride and groom are in, a pit dug by the beggars, is a tabernacle (*sukkah*). Furthermore, it is a kabbalistic custom to invite one of the seven shepherds to one's tabernacle on each of the seven days.

As I have noted, the beggars represent the seven shepherds, but the correspondence is not total either in historical order or even in kabbalistic symbolism. Nachman was not writing a commentary on the sources but was telling an allegorical tale that draws heavily on them; and one should not seek consistent or rigid equivalences here. The figures are composite and sometimes conflated.

THE BLIND BEGGAR'S TALE

Each beggar's tale is introduced by a standard formula: On arrival at the wedding feast the beggar declares his intention of completing the blessing that he had bestowed on the children in the forest, a gift that has existed only in potential and is now to be made effective. He explains the paradoxical nature of his deformity and then goes on to tell about the storytelling competition in which each participant claims the greatest prowess in a particular quality. The blind beggar's tale differs from the others in that it offers a partial commentary on its own symbolism.

The blind beggar is symbolic of the patriarch Isaac, who in the biblical account is characterized by both blindness and a long life. The beggar explains to the children that his blindness is in fact an acuity of vision so great that he does not perceive the details of mundane existence and sees everything in the perspective of eternity. The competition by which he proves his superiority to the others also deals with eternity or the length of life. The problem of time greatly preoccupied Nachman, and he discussed various aspects of it in his writings. The duration of time, in his doctrine, is not mathematically measured in years, months, and hours, but rather in terms of the content and the significance of the events that fill it. Hence the great importance of memory. Furthermore, there are different kinds of time. In the higher levels of existence, in the upper worlds, duration is progressively more concentrated; and as one reaches the highest realms, it contracts to a single dot that verges on nothingness.

Certain details are omitted in the eagle's explanation of the various stories, including, of course, the significance of his own role. In fact, the eagle is a representation of the kabbalistic figure known as the "prince of the world" or the "youth." Nachman portrays him as possessing the same characteristic as the blind beggar, a combination of great youth and great age. One of the tasks of the prince of the world is to bring to the souls of the dead tidings that the Resurrection is at hand, and that their bodies will be reconstituted. The eagle himself and the blind beggar have reached such a high degree of "timelessness" that they have loosened their ties to physical existence.

The sea on which the people in the blind beggar's story were sailing is life in this world, and the ships are their bodies. The tempest, as in other tales, is the force of evil: here it is death, which can destroy the body but not the soul. The tower is the Garden of Eden, according to a kabbalistic doctrine that states that the souls of the dead reside there in anticipation of the resurrection of their bodies. Implicit here is the fact that both the eagle and the blind beggar exist at a spiritual level where the body is not very important. The first gift, then, that the bride and groom receive is an acuity of vision associated with a perception of eternity.

THE DEAF BEGGAR

Unlike the blind beggar, the deaf beggar states explicitly that his gift is not his apparent deformity but a related quality —that is, the good life he lives. The connection between the two is simpler in this tale than in the previous one. The beggar's deafness is in fact his inability to hear the vanities and the troubles of the world, and his gift is a "good life"—that is, a life without troubles.

On the level of biblical symbolism, this beggar represents the patriarch Abraham, who is said to have had "a good life." In Genesis 24:1 it is said, "And the Lord had blessed Abraham in all things," and one midrashic source alludes to him as "the deaf servant of the Lord."

In various places in his works, Nachman refers to the phenomenon of noise. He states that worldly sounds have no real existence. He refers not only to the cries of pain that derive from want but also to the sounds uttered by men when they think they are enjoying true abundance but are in fact in the intermediate stage of the temporary relief afforded by the gratification of ephemeral needs. The true *zaddik*, who lives a good life, must thus be deaf and must pay no attention either to the imaginary problems of life or to its illusory pleasures. The nature of the good life is the topic of the deaf beggar's tale.

The garden is the collectivity of human souls, and it contains all fragrances, colors, and forms. The gardener is the *zaddik* of the generation, whose task is to take care of the souls both individually and communally. As long as he is present, the inhabitants can live a good life; but when he leaves, everything begins to disintegrate, and the evil king—the powers of evil or man's evil inclination—takes over. It is interesting to note that evil cannot destroy the garden but can only corrupt it. The fact that the inhabitants of the garden cannot withstand evil indicates the superficiality of the good life they had previously enjoyed, whether one of physical or spiritual riches.

The people of the land of great wealth, who ostensibly live a good life and who set out to save the garden, are unable to resist the pervasive corruption and have to be rescued by the bread and water of the beggar. Their riches, which are spiritual as well as material, are superficial; and only the true good life of the beggar—a minimal relating to the world, or partial deafness—is effective.

The beggar's diagnosis of the ills of the garden and his prescription of techniques to overcome them are derived largely from traditional and hasidic sources. The people of the garden have been corrupted by moral vices, personified by the bands of slaves. The way to conquer these vices is to understand their origins. Once one has achieved a basic awareness of the nature of one's evil inclinations, one can start to eliminate them and to move toward a general rehabilitation. After taking such a step, the people of the garden are once again able to recognize the gardener, the *zaddik* of the generation, and Redemption is brought nearer.

THE BEGGAR WHO STUTTERED

The third beggar's tale is one of the most famous tales in all hasidic, as well as in world religious, literature. Its remarkably few images are employed with great poetic skill and conjure up a substantial, almost palpable mystical world.

The beggar who stuttered represents Moses, who was described in the Bible as "slow of speech, and of a slow tongue." Moses attained a higher spiritual level than any other human being who ever lived, and his understanding of the Torah transcended all its interpretations. As a result his speech was so lofty that other men could hear only fragments of it. In its wholeness and perfection Moses' speech was a close approximation to the truth of divine diction, whereas the speech of other men, even of prophets, was partial and relative.

The wisdom of the various sages the beggar mentions at the beginning of the tale is inferior to his, for it concerns small, limited facets of creation. Furthermore, with the exception of the sage who is "as wise as the day," this wisdom is scientific knowledge that relates only to the understanding and the exploitation of the physical, not the metaphysical, world. The wisdom of the beggar who stuttered, on the other hand, is able to bridge the material and the divine. There is a certain thematic and a literary connection between the wisdom of this beggar and the tale of the heart and the spring.

The imagery that describes the wisdom of the last sage and that of the beggar is derived from the Kabbalah. God created the world in a series of utterances ("and God said"), each of which was made on one of the six days. In Jewish mystical

sources, these utterances and days are equated and are tanta-
mount to the vitality that maintains the world in existence. The
scientific sages are in contact with minute aspects of the totality
of Creation—hours, minutes, or seconds—whereas the sage who
is "as wise as the day" can comprehend everything created on
one of the six days. He can perceive and understand not only
details but also a significant part of God's design. The beggar,
on the other hand, can relate to any day of the divine utterances
he wishes; his wisdom encompasses the totality of the Creation.
Furthermore, implicit in the tale is his awareness of both the
totality of time and the uniqueness of each individual minute—
that is, the nonrepetitive nature of time.

The story of the heart and the spring draws on the imagery
of the Psalms, especially Psalm 61. The heart and the spring,
which are at opposite ends of the earth, are the two poles of
existence. The heart is the *Shekhinah,* the indwelling presence
of God in the world which imbues everything with life and
vitality. The spring, on the other hand, is the infinitely distant
transcendent aspect of God, the primal source from which all
divinity emanates. The heart yearns perpetually to return to
and be reunited with its origin, the first cause, but it cannot.
The burning sun and the shade given by the wings of the bird
represent, respectively, the exhausting earthly passions that
obscure true spiritual desires, and the divine grace that occasionally appears in the world.

The unbridgeable gulf between the heart and the spring, the
Shekhinah and the primal source, is a basic feature of Creation.
Were the heart ever to attempt to cross it, the world would
cease to exist. Distance from the primal source is thus a prior
condition of existence, and an intense, unending yearning
characterizes the basic relationship that inheres in the world.
However, this yearning is not entirely static but involves a kind
of ebb and flow in which the world (and man) moves toward
the transcendent, thereby nullifying its own existence temporarily before returning to mundane reality.

The depiction of the spring's dependence on the heart (the latter must provide the former with time) is a beautiful literary rendering of one of the basic tenets of the Kabbalah, according to which the world was created in a spontaneous act of grace, but its continued existence depends upon men raising up and returning some of the divine abundance. The primal source exists in nondifferentiated, and thus nonexistent, time. The world returns to it particularized moments of time, each of which is characterized by the events it contains. According to the Kabbalah, it is the holy deeds of men—in thought, in speech, and in the *mitzvot*—that maintain the world in existence, and the Torah, the blueprint of creation, that lays down the way these are to be performed. The Torah is the covenant between the world and God; when man obeys its precepts, the Creation is renewed from moment to moment.

Thus the beggar who stuttered, Moses, the man of the Torah, can fill such an essential role in the world. He is the true *zaddik*, the intermediary, who passes on to the man of true grace—who himself represents one of the aspects of God—the sparks of holiness raised in the world.

THE BEGGAR WITH THE CROOKED NECK

The fourth beggar represents the biblical Aaron, brother of Moses and first priest of Israel. In midrashic and esoteric literature Aaron is described as the "best man" of the *Shekhinah*, and his task is to reunite Israel with God. Music, the theme of this beggar's tale, is symbolic of the creation of harmony, the discovery of the inner connection between things and their drawing together. The musicians with whom the beggar competes are capable of creating harmony only to a limited degree, as their inability to help the two countries shows. They cannot cure the pain of the world. The two countries afflicted with insuperable sorrow are as far apart as heaven and earth, and the two birds (whose image is derived largely from a kabbalistic interpretation of the symbolism of the two winged cherubim in the Temple) are symbolic of God and the *Shekhinah,* who, as was noted in previous stories, is somewhat equivalent to *Knesset Israel,* the quintessential community of Israel. When the Temple was still standing, the two lived together in perfect bliss; but since the Exile they have been separated and yearn unceasingly for each other.

By day, the sorrow of the two birds is alleviated by the singing of the other birds, which symbolizes the prayer and rejoicing of human souls. At dusk, however, grief becomes the predominant factor in the world; Jewish literature is replete with references to the nightly weeping of God and the *Shekhinah* over the bitterness of the Exile.

It should be noted that although the beggar knows how to bring the two birds together, the tale does not state that he actually does this. The reason is simple. Reuniting the birds is equivalent to bringing about the Redemption, which no one beggar can do. The Redemption will come only when the powers of all the beggars are brought together in a single person (or in the bride and groom).

THE HUNCHBACKED BEGGAR

The fifth beggar is representative of the patriarch Jacob, who in postbiblical literature is described as the pillar that supports the entire structure of all the worlds. The hunched back of the beggar, which can apparently bear nothing, is in fact symbolic of the opposite, the power of the "little that holds the great," the capacity of a small object to contain a great abundance. On a metaphysical level, it is the ability to control the world or to perceive the infinite within the finite.

The competition among the various people who all claim to possess this power exposes various common fallacies concerning its significance. The first competitor, who is ridiculed in an almost Swiftian satire, makes the mistake of seeing the ability to contain the great within the little as no more than the concentration of a particular quality. He is incapable of changing its essence and certainly has acquired no control over it.

The man with the small plot of land producing a large quantity of crops can be seen as someone who performs the *mitzvot,* which contain within them the great yield of their rewards. The orchard of the next competitor can perhaps be seen as the Torah, which possesses many deep levels of significance in addition to the simple meaning of the text. The secretary is a kind of sage and *zaddik* who is able to compose, on behalf of others, prayers to God in which he includes the collective desires of mankind. Silence is the ability to change the nature of, and thus overcome, the destructive aspects of human speech.

In the Kabbalah the moon is always regarded as symbolic of the *Shekhinah.* It has "no light of its own," just as the *Shekhinah* derives all nourishment from the higher *Sefirot.* As has been noted frequently, the *Shekhinah* needs the deeds of men to function in the world. The man who leads the "huge blind man" is thus symbolic of a great *zaddik,* a man who directs human activity and helps the *Shekhinah.*

Whereas other beggars' tales dealt with the problem of time, the emphasis here is on space. The place in which all space is focused is the Tree of Life, whose description in the Book of Daniel (4:7–9) is reflected in the imagery of the tree in this tale. All creatures derive their life from this tree and seek to find it. It is not easily found, however, for it is located at a point that contains the essence of all space. Even before the people in the tale set out on their quest, they discover that the location of the tree is characterized by a further, nonspatial dimension, that of mortality, and that to prepare themselves they must develop the qualities of faith in God, humility, and truth. When they have done this, differences of opinion, which derive from relating to the material world, disappear.

Just as the source of time exists outside time, so the essence of space is not to be found within the boundaries and limitations of this world. The differentiation of space into separate places implies the presence of contradictions and opposites that can only be resolved beyond the world, in infinity. However, though the moral qualities acquired by the seekers permit them to approach the tree, they do not provide the actual means to transcend the limitations of place; the people need the help of the hunchbacked beggar, the *zaddik* who can grasp the infinity of space within a single point, who can hold the great within the small. This ability is the gift the beggar bestows upon the bride and groom.

THE BEGGAR WITH NO HANDS

The beggar with no hands represents the biblical Joseph, who is known in postbiblical books as the *zaddik*. This beggar possesses many of the characteristics of the hasidic *zaddik*, especially the ability to act on the material world. He has the power to save the princess—the *Shekhinah*—from her suffering and thereby to heal the pain of the world.

The people who boast about the strength of their hands possess certain aspects of the spiritual powers that have been mastered in their entirety by the beggar, and that are qualities of the hasidic *zaddik*. The retrieval of an arrow even after it has struck its prey is symbolic of the process of repentance, which can reverse and negate an act that has already taken place. By repenting, one creates a situation in which it is as if the evil deed that one has committed no longer exists. The ten different kinds of arrow represent sins connected with the ten

Sefirot—or, rather, with their counterparts, the ten *Sefirot* of impurity or of evil. Only a true *zaddik* is able to bring about repentance for all kinds of sin.

The dispensation of charity acquired a special meaning in the hasidic movement. The *zaddik* was generally supported financially by his followers, to whom in return he gave spiritual nourishment and guidance. This relationship was frequently likened to that between the Sabbath, "the source of blessing," and the weekdays, which "give it charity" and thereby receive sustenance. The receiving that is also giving is thus characteristic of the *zaddik*.

The bestowal of wisdom, which here also signifies spiritual energy, was another of the functions of the *zaddik*. In the Zohar and other kabbalistic works it is stated that the truly righteous can know the state of a man's wisdom and his needs by feeling his pulse. Furthermore, the *zaddik* could understand and redirect the evil impulse of his followers, here represented by the ten different kinds of raging wind that can be converted into sweet melodies.

The tale of the princess and the evil king is another version of the first story in this volume. The princess is a symbolic representation of the *Shekhinah*, the soul of the world; the king, of the forces of evil. His passion for her reflects the desire of evil to unite with holiness and to derive from it the flow of divine abundance. This is possible, and it does happen—but only temporarily, for eventually the evil will be defeated by the very good that it enslaves. The imagery in this story is strongly reminiscent of the biblical account of the Exodus. Pharaoh ruled over the children of Israel and grew progressively suspicious and fearful of them. The water here represents the Red Sea, through which the Jews passed safely, but in which Pharaoh and his host were drowned.

Symbolically the castle of water is divine wisdom, or the wisdom of the Torah, which is often referred to as water. Only the true *zaddik* can penetrate its miraculous liquid walls, the depths of esoteric wisdom, and can cure the mortally injured princess, the *Shekhinah*. We are not told that the beggar actually does this. As in the tale of the beggar with the crooked neck, the gift exists potentially and can be brought to actuality only when it is bestowed upon the bride and groom.

CONCLUSION

Not only is the *Shekhinah* not saved at the end of the sixth tale, but also there is no conclusion to the story as a whole. The seventh beggar, who has no feet, has not arrived at the wedding, and we are not told what happens to the king's son with whom the story begins. Nachman himself stated that he did not wish to conclude this tale, which would in fact have ended with the Redemption. It is, nevertheless, possible to follow through a number of hints in the text and other sources to see what might happen.

The beggar with no feet is representative of the biblical King David, whose dancing is described in Chapter 6 of the second book of Samuel. Dancing was of great significance in the hasidic movement, and the role it played in hasidic celebrations is vividly portrayed in many written accounts. Dance, in bringing together all the powers of the feet, represents the basis of simple and perfect faith. A further association with this image is the period immediately preceding the arrival of the Messiah, which is called "the footsteps of the Messiah." When the bride and groom receive the gift of the seventh beggar, they will have acquired the degrees of perfection of each of the seven shepherds and will be able to go on to their own day, the day of the Messiah. Then they will be able to save the king's son from his doubts and will themselves assume rule of the land, and perfection will be restored to the world.